A WOMAN'S WORTH & WORK

A WOMAN'S WORTH & WORK

A CHRISTIAN PERSPECTIVE

KAREN HELDER De VOS

BAKER BOOK HOUSE
Grand Rapids, Michigan

With love and gratitude
to my mother
because she is proud of my achievements,
she refuses to tolerate self-pity,
she listened, and listened, and still listens,
and to Peter
because his love supports me always —
in anger, joy, frustration,
contentment, chaos, and peace

Preface

The women's movement, or the feminist movement, is one of the most talked-about and written-about social issues of our time. Nearly every magazine, including those with specifically Christian concerns, has had articles on that subject in the last two years. But there is no single writing by a Christian that sorts out the main issues from the peripheral ones, and suggests to what extent a Christian can, or should, be accepting and working for the goals of the movement. In this book I hope to do these two things.

The feminist movement can be very loosely divided into the moderate and the radical branches. The radicals are much the smaller of the two groups, though they receive more attention from the mass media. Radicals want to revise the entire social and/or economic structure of the nation. These are the feminists who talk of abolishing the nuclear family because it is the chief support of a competitive economic system of which they disapprove. They talk of communal marriage, breaking down the capitalist system, and the legitimacy of lesbianism.

The moderate section of the movement wants none of these things. Moderate feminists wish to get women into the existing economic system; they do not wish to build a different system. They want women in government, in business, in all areas of contemporary life. They are not interested in the destruction of the family or in eliminating the usual sexual attraction between male and female. They want equality, not unisex. They would like to see a change of roles for men and women, not the abolishment of men. These are the feminists whose goals I will be describing in chapter one.

The radical and moderate groups, naturally, are not always clearly distinguishable. Rather, they are general groupings in which there is some overlapping.

Christians are frequently attracted to the goals of feminism but feel that such goals are contrary to what they have been taught by Scripture. In chapter two, I will summarize some of the interpretations that feminists have offered of the "women" passages in the Bible. And in chapter three, I will evaluate how a Christian should respond to the goals of the moderate feminists.

Contents

CHAPTER THREE

CHAPTER
ONE

What Do Feminists Want?

Critics of the current feminist movement frequently act as if the women in the movement are spoiled, discontented children. "What do they want?" the critics ask irritably. "They already own most of the property, can sit around the house all day, have more than 50 percent of the vote." As one television comedian put it, "My wife called the chauffeur to drive her from our twelve-room house in Yonkers to a meeting for women's liberation." His face and the audience's reaction clearly showed that women were indeed inexplicable and unreasonable.

Feminists, however, want something quite different from sitting around the house all day and having chauffeurs drive them to meetings. They do not want to take life easy or to have things given them; they do not want to be "treated better," in the sense of being waited on and cherished. They want power and respect. They are saying, "We do not want to be well-treated pets or indulged children; we want to be hard-working, professional people who get a fair share of the economic and political and power-structure pie." It should not be difficult for a man to understand that desire. The comedian who made that comment also has a chauffeur and a house in Yonkers and enough money to keep those things the rest of his life. Yet he goes on working. The men who complain so irritably that they can't understand what women want are the same men who last week or last month took on another committee assignment, or a more difficult job, or another directorship. Those men surely do not want to sit around their offices all day; they surely are not content with mere money. They want power, influence, and success (however they define that term); they want to feel that they've accomplished something in this world.

When asked why he was investing energy and money in yet another business enterprise, an extremely wealthy Christian businessman put it very well: "A man needs a challenge."

Women, too, say the feminists, need a challenge. And while housekeeping and bringing up children may be a challenge to some women, it is not a challenge to all, anymore than the businessman's desire to make money seems challenging to the scholar, or the scholar's desire to find exactly the right reading of an ancient manuscript seems challenging to a truck driver.

Feminists are not merely discontented with their own lots in life; they are discontented with the way lots in life are distributed, that is, by sex. They are not saying only that women get a raw deal; they are also saying that the chief criterion for distributing deals, sex, is a bad one and ought to be changed. They are saying that whatever relevance sex once had to decide that women stayed home to nurse babies and men went out to kill the food, its relevance is gone. Roles and learned characteristics and expectations about people should no longer be based on sex.

This is the underlying principle in almost all feminist demands: sex should not be considered and is not relevant in almost all of the cases where it is currently considered, either consciously or unconsciously, a criterion. Thus in the past there was, it seemed, some reason why women were better telephone operators than men; that distinction has proved false and men now man some telephone lines. There was also, apparently, some reason why men were better suited to be surgeons or car salesmen or executives. False, say the feminists; if women were allowed the chance, they would prove to be just as good at those jobs as the men are. The same assumption underlies the complaints about women being treated as sex objects, about women being treated as underlings socially, about women being expected to stay home with the children. In each of these cases, say the feminists, women are being thought of or judged in certain ways because of their sex, a criterion which simply is not relevant.

14

Let us examine in more detail precisely what feminists want. In any large and widespread movement there are differences of opinion among its adherents, of course. Feminists range from radicals who want to abolish marriage and the nuclear family to gentle housewives who want only to assert their right to turn off the football game during Sunday dinner. In speaking of what feminists want, I will try to make clear the goals for which there is widespread interest, and some of the major variations within the movement.

The reader should remember that in describing these desires, I am not endorsing them nor claiming that any Christian could or should endorse them; I am merely saying *what* feminists want. In chapter three I will take up the problem of how Christians should respond to these demands.

1. Equality in Jobs

The most universally accepted goal among feminists is that of equal job opportunities and equal pay for equal work. The extent of discrimination against women has been documented elsewhere[1] and its existence has been accepted by every student of the evidence. The fact has been established that women are discriminated against, both in the jobs they are allowed to hold and in the pay they receive for their work.

For one example of how this works, take the female secretary to the president of a small college. She may be, by the president's own admission, his "right-hand" in the running of the place. It may be quite obvious to everyone in the college that her absence, more than that of anyone else, is more disruptive to the smooth running of the college. Yet she will undoubtedly remain a "secretary" and receive secretary's wages the entire time she is employed there. If a man were, by some fluke, to become "secretary" to the president, as many men are to political figures, and he were to become invaluable, even indispensable, he would almost certainly be given the title "assistant to the president" and be given his *own* secretary to do menial tasks such as typing and filing. And his salary would immediately be made commensurate with his position as assistant to the president. That is the kind of discrimination that has been documented over and over again in studies on job opportunities for women. The point is that women frequently are doing

---

[1] Most copiously in *Discrimination Against Women,* a two-volume transcript of the Hearings before the Special Committee on Education of the Committee on Education and Labor, House of Representatives, 91st Congress, July 1 and 31, 1970.

More readably in Caroline Bird, *Born Female,* (New York, 1968).

exactly the same work as men, but because the work is labeled differently, they are expected to work for lower wages.

Other kinds of discrimination have been documented also. Women are not given equal consideration for promotion. When several clerks are working in an office and an opening occurs for an office manager, the job almost invariably is given to a man; frequently the possibility of appointing one of the women never even occurs to the people in power. Especially in jobs where certain managerial skills are involved, the rationale is that none of the women have the right kind of ability or the right emotional make-up, or sometimes that the men would not work well under a woman. All of these arguments are mere rationalizations, say the feminists, the same ones that were used to discriminate against blacks for many years. When women have been appointed to such jobs, they have functioned just as well as men, and men very quickly learn to work under a woman if it is made clear that their only alternative to doing so is to find another job.

Even clearer forms of discrimination have been documented. Factories where women are automatically paid less than men are not uncommon. In fact, some industries have been forced by court order to grant women back pay to make up for what the court felt was a sexual distinction made among workers. Even more common are industrial examples of our first case: factories where the apparent reason for wage differentials is that the jobs are different, but where the real reason is that some jobs are reserved for men and others are held by women.

The oft-cited statistic that women have poorer work records than men is not fair, say the feminists, because it usually pits the work records of women in menial jobs which they care little about against the work records of men in jobs that are important to them. The business executive who says he wouldn't appoint a woman sales manager because his secretaries have such poor records is guilty of such a mistake. Rather, let him look at the work records of women who have been given responsible jobs, women who do care about their work and are not merely marking time until they get married. In those cases, say the feminists, with evidence to document their statement, women's work records are just as good as men's. A look at the records of teachers would be one easy way to make such a check. Furthermore, say the feminists, one cannot just ask the person in charge about such things; actual records must be examined. Otherwise, the prejudices of the person answering may be coloring his reply.

Still further, assert the feminists, even if the records do show greater absences of women in responsible positions, much of the reason is that the women are expected by their husbands to carry most of the responsibility for the home and children. If a water pipe breaks as both are going off to work, it is quite likely the woman who will stay home to await the plumber, thereby having a tardy arrival on her record. And if one of the children is sick, it is she who is expected to make a change in her schedule to meet the emergency. If men were to take equal responsibility for the family, as is only fair if the woman is working full-time, the work records would not show disproportionate absences for women.

Women are demanding, then, equal opportunity in jobs, promotions, and wages. But "equal opportunity" is a slippery phrase. Is equal opportunity produced by an end to conscious discrimination after generations of deliberate, even legal, discrimination? The feminists say no. They say that compensatory steps must be taken to give a different image of the formerly subjected group and that certain institutions will need to be established or changed in order to make equal opportunity a reality.

2. Abortion on Demand

Some women base their case for abortion-on-demand on equal opportunity grounds. A woman cannot have genuinely equal opportunity to pursue a career, they claim, unless she has total control over when or if she will bear children. Until a completely safe method of birth control, one without side effects, is produced, women need the option of abortion to make the possibility of careers a reality. Nearly all feminists agree on the need for freely chosen abortion, but not all use this argument. Some argue that women have the "right to control their own bodies"; others base their demand on the premises that men cannot understand or appreciate the problem women face in bearing a child and that therefore legislatures, committees of medical doctors, or hospital committees have no right to make such decisions because they are dominated by men. I have never found a feminist writer (though that does not mean none exists) who took seriously the position that the fetus has rights as well as the pregnant woman. We will return to this subject in chapter three.

3. An End of Stereotypes

Women can do only certain jobs

The need to change the images of women is widely accepted as preliminary to genuine equality of opportunity. Not only do men need their images of women changed, say the feminists, but also women have an image of themselves as inferior or as incompetent in certain areas. Women have absorbed, have internalized as the psychologists say, the image of them projected in books, magazines, films, and television. They have come to believe in the feminine image concocted by the mass media. Thus girls don't *expect* to do well in mathematics or science courses, are surprised if they do, and still do not project the possibility of making that their life's work. If asked why, they would not say "No women do that sort of work," but the feeling is nonetheless that it is unfeminine or masculine to do certain things. Examine your own image of a woman who decides to become a highway engineer, for example. You will be surprised if she turns out to be a slim, attractive thing with all the qualities usually associated with womanhood.

There is furthermore the problem of girls having models after which to pattern themselves. That all of us use models in determining our goals in life is well accepted. For girls, there are no models other than those of unmarried career women or wives and mothers with, possibly, part-time jobs. A girl is likely to know few women who have successfully combined motherhood with a full-time, serious career, and therefore does not consider that combination in thinking about her future. (One possible exception here is the married school teacher, and many girls project that as their future, probably because of their exposure to this career/mother-hood example.) Mothers who are aware of this limited model problem have pointed out how difficult it is to get their daughters to consider medical school rather than nursing school, for example, because the daughter doesn't know any woman who has successfully combined the roles of physician, wife, and mother.

In order to change this image feminists demand that textbooks no longer depict women only as mothers or schoolteachers, but rather show them in the full range of occupations. Children are conditioned from their earliest storybooks and television programs, say the feminists, to the idea that women stay home with children while men do the work of the world. The doctors and newspaper editors and firemen and policemen and mailmen are all *men*. By the time they are in kindergarten many girls will tell you they want to be "mommies" when they grow up; you almost never hear a boy say he wants to be a father. The reason is simple: if you are a mother, you are nothing else. If you are a father, you have some other important work as well.

Women inherently have certain character traits

Besides being stereotyped into job roles by these early childhood associations, women and girls are also represented as being of certain character types. Women are passive, helpless, fearful, and lacking in physical abilities. The boys are always down the firemen's pole before the girls, they always win the races, they always help their little sisters get away from the big dogs. Almost never in children's storybooks does a big sister help her brother when he is scared. The boys in the stories play baseball and football while the girls play house and dolls. In some kindergartens the boys are not even *permitted* in the play house, though in most their exclusion is by peer pressure ("that's girls' play" say the other little boys, and the boy who may be fascinated by baking and cooking at home promptly pretends he thinks those activities are silly).

Further stereotyping occurs in athletics. From second or third grade on, team sports for boys are encouraged. Girls' athletics always get less attention and generally do not become fully organized activities until junior high. Even then, the coaching and the equipment for the girls' teams are nearly always inferior. At this writing, a Michigan city is fighting in court a ruling that girls may not be admitted to little league baseball. Feminists do not claim that women could be just as good in athletics as men; rather they assert that athletics is a prime example of how certain activities are almost entirely turned over to a certain sex, long before it is necessary or desirable to make such distinctions.

If it would be a good thing for girls to develop the things that sports develop — coordination, stamina, team spirit — then female sports must be taken just as seriously as male.

Women are inferior

From whatever source they learn it, by the time children are eight years old, the boys believe, or more accurately perhaps, *want* to believe in their own superiority. They are horrified if the girls beat them at anything. The competition between the two groups is encouraged, frequently, by teachers who pit them against each other, and by athletic programs that treat the two separately. It is not at all unusual to hear young boys saying with vehemence, "Girls can't play football!" And what is a girl to reply to that? "Boys can't scrub floors"? Who wants to scrub floors? Feminists would like to see this competition destroyed, not only because the girls almost always come to think of themselves as inferior, but because it is unhealthy for the boys to grow up thinking of themselves as being "better" than another whole group of people.

Boys, in fact, may suffer from this competitiveness more than girls, for somehow their sense of their own worth comes to rest on being better than the girls. And when a boy isn't better, he is unable to say simply "One person is better than I am," rather it is always, "A *girl* is better than I am," with the clear implication that he must be really inadequate. Girls seldom say, with that tone of disgust, "I was beaten by a *boy*." Some feminists believe that this early need to be better than the girls is what causes men to marry women who are inferior to them in some way, whether educationally, intellectually, or socially.

Women "should be" beautiful

The desire to change the image of women, both to themselves and to men, is also behind such demands as the feminist insistence that businesses stop using sex, especially female sex, to sell their products. The airline advertisements that said "I'm Barbara, fly me," for example, suggest that the sex appeal of the stewardess is what she has to offer, rather than good service, good food, or good conversation. The constant use of sex appeal to sell products is too obvious to anyone who looks at television or reads magazines to need documenting here.

The entire emphasis on cosmetics and on looking young is also guilty of furthering this stereotype, say the feminists. As long as our society thinks that eighteen or twenty-one is the ideal age for a woman, and that a woman is "taking care of herself" if she looks twenty when she is thirty or forty, women will feel they must spend thousands of dollars on cosmetics and hairstyling in order to attract or keep the men whose approval they want. Again, the reason that youth is considered so desirable, say the women in the movement, is that the woman is looked at as chiefly a sex object. If she were considered an intellectual companion, or an equal to be consulted in making important decisions, or a good mother, nobody would want an eighteen-year-old; they would want somebody with as much wisdom and maturity as they could find.

Ironically, just as women are beginning to object to this use of themselves as sex objects, men are beginning to indulge in it. Men, too, are now encouraged to color their grey hair, to hide their baldness, even to wear make-up in some cases. Hair spray and cologne for men are common and hairstyling salons, as opposed to old fashioned barber shops, are doing good business. Burt Reynolds' appearance in the centerfold of *Cosmopolitan* is the exemplar of this trend. Feminists do not approve of such goings-on for men any more than for women. People should not be treated as beautiful or ugly objects, they insist, nor judged by their physical appearance.

Refusal to accept the usual standard of feminine beauty is a large item on the feminist agenda, then. Feminists demand that age in a woman be just as acceptable as age in a man (perhaps more accurately, as age in a man *used* to be), that women refuse to play the game of trying to look younger and more glamorous than they are, that they refuse to spend disproportionately large segments of their time and money and energy keeping their skins and bodies in top condition. In short, they want women to concern themselves more with the inside and less with the outside of themselves.

Women must marry

Closely related to this image of youth and sex appeal is the feeling girls have that they must find a man. The single life is the worst thing they can imagine; it is a reflection of failure in the most important area of a girl's life, that of being attractive to men. The concern starts as early as fourteen or fifteen. Women, mothers, are the most guilty of perpetuating this foolish concern. They often prefer their daughters to marry at eighteen, in spite of divorce statistics on teen-age marriages, just to know that the daughters won't be "old maids." An unmarried daughter of twenty-four becomes almost a skeleton in the family closet, at least for the mother. If a daughter goes off to school or work in another city, the most frequent question the mother will hear is, "Has she met any nice young man yet?" Feminists wish to change this attitude. They wish to make the decision to remain single a respectable one that does not carry with it an aura of failure. The feminists wish to make concern for becoming an independent, mature per-

24

son instead of interest in attracting a man the number-one priority of women.

Women should live by men's sexual expectations

Sexual relationships between men and women used to be regulated by the belief that a man could and would go so far as the woman let him, and it was her job, if she was a "nice" girl, to make sure marriage (at the least, the promise of marriage) preceded her loss of virginity. Current attitudes toward sex have changed all this. Girls are now supposed to be just as interested in sex as boys, women are expected to enjoy the swinging life of promiscuity as much as men. But, say many feminists, women are still trapped by their own desire to please the men. Girls used to feel obligated to pretend virginity whether they had it or not; now they feel obligated to pretend experience, or at the least, a desire for experience, if they are virgins. In either case, say the feminists, the woman is trying to please the man rather than living by her own desires and needs.

Women can't think

Another stereotype that many people have about women is that they are inherently less rational than men. Even if the accepted stereotype of how women think is an accurate representation, the question of why they behave this way is still unanswered. Is the behavior something inherent in women, or is it the result of conditioning by their society?

Whatever may appear to the casual observer to be the case, researchers have been testing for over fifty years to try to discover correlations between sex and inherent intelligence. They have consistently been unable to do so. They have been unable even to correlate sex with such *apparently* sex-linked areas as mathematics and science. All the evidence points to the fact that women are in no way different from men in their thinking processes; that whatever differences may appear in practical situations are the result of societal pressures.

Housework belongs to females

Still another sterotype that feminists wish to destroy is the belief that housework is woman's work, regardless of what else the wife does. So ingrained is the idea that cleaning, washing, ironing, and bedmaking are female tasks that even women who are working fulltime are expected to carry on these household tasks. A chemistry professor who was washing his own test tubes once commented to me that he needed a *lady* around to do his dishes for him. Even among graduate students whose wives are supporting them, any help with this work is considered a contribution made out of the goodness of the male heart, not an obligation incurred in exchange for having his wife support him. Shopping and cooking are somewhat less strongly identified as female tasks; when a husband offers to share the housework, he almost always takes on one of these chores.

Even if a woman does decide to make marriage and motherhood her full-time job for a time, she should not become her husband's maid, say the feminists. Spending her whole day caring for a house and children ought not be extended into responsibility for her husband's wardrobe, picking up after him, jumping up from the table to supply his needs. There is no reason for a woman to feel "He's had a hard day," and must be waited on, if she has spent the day caring for children and house. Motherhood must not be confused with the idea that a woman's place is to wait on her man, to make every meal for him, to pick up his coffee cups, to clean his ashtrays, to press his pants, to run his errands.

Feminists frequently blame this maid-syndrome on the Christian (or Judeo-Christian) teaching that a woman should be a helpmeet for a man. We will take up that matter further in chapter two; let me just say here that there is no reason a helpmeet's help has to be in the form of menial tasks such as sorting socks and getting the rings out of collars.

Women "should be" happy as housewives

A further problem that feminists often lay at the door of the church is women's guilt over wanting to have their own lives. Christianity, they claim, has taught passivity and subjection and service for women to such an extent that women are afraid to admit that living for and through their husbands and children is not enough for them. Whatever the cause of the problem, the guilt level among women is very high. The working mothers feel guilty that they do not stay home with the children; many women have practically stumbled over their words in their haste to assure me that working (even part time) makes them better mothers. The working wives feel guilty over asking their husbands to take on any responsibility or chore that wives "should" do; they assure me that they still get up to fix their husbands' breakfasts, in spite of full-time obligations. And many of the wives and mothers who do stay home feel guilty that they can't be happier in doing so.

One stereotype that the feminists have destroyed without particularly intending to, is the myth of the happy housewife. That is not to say that there are no happy housewives, but their number is fewer than the mass media would make one think. Betty Freidan's *The Feminine Mystique* (New York, 1963) documents the problem thoroughly. Over and over again she found women saying, "I should be happy; I have a good husband, lovely children, a beautiful home, but lots of nights I just sit and cry," or "I think about commiting suicide," or "I dream of running away to the city to work." Yet these women cannot break out of their traps, partly because they do not realize the problem is not in them, but in their lifestyles. But even if they did realize it, they would feel too guilty about leaving the children to demand the right to work at something they find meaningful and fulfilling.

To say that such women *ought* to be happy is ridiculous, say the feminists. They are clear proof that many women simply do not find the role of wife and mother totally satisfying. They ought to be doing something else, and doing it without guilt.

4. Alternate Child Care

Some feminists include among their goals the total abolishment of housewife status. They say it is debilitating to be dependent on another person, the way a housewife is on her husband, for total support, either financial or emotional. They claim that dependency keeps women emotional children, keeps them from growing into their full possibilities as people. They assert that keeping house, whether with or without children, is such a boring, repetitive, uncreative job that no one should be doing it as her chief end in life.

Other feminists feel that monogamy is unnatural or too restraining and advocate, on those grounds, an end to marriage. Still others say that any relationship which is not entirely "free" is not an honest one; they wish to abolish marriage in favor of a come-and-go-when-it-suits-you arrangement of living together. Others advocate communal marriage. Perhaps the most radical, in terms of relationships between men and women, are those who claim that no man in this culture can possibly allow a woman freedom and self-identity. Therefore they advocate satisfaction of sexual desire through masturbation or lesbianism.

But the most common position among feminists is that marriage is a good thing, that families are good things, that we should do what we can to preserve the family and to prevent divorce, provided those things can be done without destroying the abilities or self-esteem of women. Most feminists would not insist that no woman should be a full-time housewife. Most of them would say that this should, like any career, be a choice open to those who are inclined in that direction. They would, in fact, like to open that choice to men as well. They insist that a woman must have as much choice in her career as a man has in his, and that being a mother should not limit a woman's choice any more than being a father limits a man's. To that end, they advocate various means.

The most immediate demand is for maternity leave on the order of sick leave. Feminists differ in the length of leave they want and on whether it should be paid or unpaid, but the usual demand is for three months' leave with return to the job assured without loss of benefits or seniority. Just as men are given leave if they have heart attacks or ulcer problems, and national guardsmen must be given two weeks each summer, so women should be permitted their three months' maternity leave without retribution. Complaints about how disruptive it would be for a business to have its employees gone for three months are met immediately by a reference to the fact that men, with their higher heart attack rates, are still considered employable. Feminists are quick to point out that when men do have heart attacks or back problems or ulcers, they are given sick leave. Furthermore, more and more businesses are sending their executives back to school or training institutes for extended periods; if businesses can do that, they can manage maternity leaves. It isn't that businesses could not manage maternity leaves, claim the feminists; it is that they do not want to.

Once the maternity leave is over, the working mother needs a substitute to care for the baby. Feminists have several proposals to meet this need.

The most common demand is for day care centers. Some feminists maintain that every large industry or organization that acts as an employer should offer day care for employees' children. Then mother, or father for that matter, could take the preschoolers with them when they leave in the morning and turn them over to competent preschool teachers and nursery attendants until the working day is over. It is generally suggested that the cost to the employer for this service be offset by tax benefits.

Other feminists demand that day care centers be added to the public schools. The school already has the children many hours a day, many years of their lives, it has already taken over much of the responsibility for maintaining the children's health, it is already moving toward education for three- and four-year-olds; therefore it is the logical place to put day care, say those who advocate this arrangement. Such centers would have the advantage of providing after school care for older youngsters as well as care for preschoolers, and of being, as long as we have neighborhood schools at least, a community arrangement that would offer the child some continuity with his school experience. Furthermore, the buildings and equipment for after school care for older youngsters are already there and such an arrangement would offer greater use of those expensive facilities. And a funding arrangement already exists that would eliminate the need for finding some new source of funds.

Feminists who distrust the public schools, or in some cases any government-run institution, are pushing for tax credits for payments made to private day care centers. Such an arrangement would allow the parents free choice of care, giving them options among highly structured or more open arrangements, for example, and would improve the quality of day care by making it competitive. Those who want this arrangement want tax *credits* or vouchers. They will not be satisfied with being able to deduct the cost of day care from their taxable income. Like those who want state-supported centers, these feminists are insisting that the taxpayers bear the full cost of child care for working parents.

The whole issue of who should pay for child care is a complicated one. The more radical feminists argue that if a society really believes that child care is important and really wants people to take child care seriously, that society should be willing to pay for it. They maintain that whether a child is cared for at home by his mother or in a nursery of some sort by others, the people who care for him should be paid for doing so. (The more traditional view is, of course, that the family is responsible for child care and nobody gets paid for doing it.) These feminists point out that the state has an interest in getting *good* child care; without it, the state will ultimately have to deal with problems of delinquency and crime. They say that free day care is like free public education. Because society benefits from having all its members educated and because it believes in equality of opportunity for all, the state bears the cost of education. Similarly, because society would benefit by having the children receive good care and by having the mothers constructively employed, and because it is only just that mothers have equal opportunity to work, such feminists advocate that the state should also bear the cost of child care.

Other feminists propose less radical solutions to the problem, less radical at least in that they do not propose moving child care out of the home. Some claim that there are many women, and perhaps many men, who genuinely *like* to take care of small children and who do it well. These women are now forced to take factory or retail sales jobs when they return to the labor market. Such people should instead be utilized to care for the children of parents who do not want to care for their own children or who are not especially good at it. The job of mother's helper should be made a job much like the paramedical professions. There should be some training, perhaps a year's, in child psychology, in the problems that might arise because the worker is dealing with someone else's children rather than her own, in proper nutrition, in other areas that might be helpful to someone dealing with small children. At the successful conclusion of the course, the trainee would be a licensed or registered mother's helper and the mother who hires her could be certain of her competence. The pay would have to be commensurate with the training, perhaps much like the wages paid practical nurses. The pay scale and the status would be that of a professional, not just a baby-sitter. These benefits would attract people to this profession, claim the feminists. Whether or not this plan is workable nobody knows because it has not been tried.

Other means of permitting careers for mothers are advocated. A change in the law to make mothers equally responsible with fathers

32

for the support of their children is advocated by some feminists. This would encourage women to take seriously the need to prepare themselves for self-support and to maintain their skills even if they are staying at home with families for a time. Under such a law, there would be no more support for a widowed mother than for a widowed father; the mother would be expected to be self-supporting, just as widowed fathers now are. There would be no welfare specifically for mothers; there would be welfare only for *parents* who were unable to get jobs, whether male or female. Such a law would move women out of the category of dependents into the category of self-sufficient, self-supporting citizens and would, therefore, be much more just than the current laws that burden fathers with too much financial responsibility and mothers with too little sense of their own competence and independence.

Insistence that businesses, government organizations, schools, and other employers permit people to work half-time at half-pay without foregoing their rights to promotion, fringe-benefits, full employee status, and so forth, is another proposed solution. Under this plan mother and father would each work half-time while the children are young. As the children became less dependent, both parents could return to their careers full-time without having lost the seniority and benefits that would have been theirs had they been full-time employees during that period. Directors of organizations frequently maintain that such plans are unworkable, that they need their responsible people there at all times. Feminists agree that the plans are unworkable at present because arrangements are not geared to them. However, they insist that the problems *could* be met if the people in charge were serious about wanting to meet them. Once again, until such an arrangement is tried, one cannot know whether or not it will work.

To summarize, by various means feminists are proposing that the burden of child care be shared by others instead of being borne entirely by mothers. The feminists feel it is unjust that women should have to choose between careers and families, while men are routinely expected to have both. It is unjust that women's abilities and skills should shrivel and deteriorate for years while they are washing diapers and scrubbing floors. It is unjust that women should be deprived of the stimulation and creativity of work that meets their needs and abilities and that is valued by others in their society.

The case for and against these methods of child care is, among Christians, undoubtedly one of the most hotly debated of all feminist goals. Once again, we must defer the treatment of a Christian view of these goals until chapter three.

These, then, are the objectives of the mainsteam of current feminism: equal job opportunities and equal pay, abortion by choice, the destruction of stereotypes about women (and men), the development of some alternatives to the traditional method of child care; in sum, the opportunity for each woman to choose her life work rather than having it chosen for her by her sex.

Choice is the watchword of the feminists. Choice for both men and women. Choice of career, choice of whether or not to marry, choice of whether or not to have children, choice of child care arrangements when one does have children, choice in determining how the housework will be handled, choice in deciding who is responsible for what in each marriage. Abolish preordained roles, they say, abolish expectations that because of his sex a person will behave a certain way, or will perform certain tasks, or will want certain things; let each person choose his tasks and roles, let each person follow his abilities without concern for sexual stereotypes, let each develop according to personal need rather than society's pressure.

CHAPTER
TWO

What Does the Bible Say?

One large difficulty Christians have with agreeing with the goals of the women's movement is that they genuinely believe the Bible makes contrary claims. Feminists are inclined to believe that most of the argument against their goals is mere chauvinism and self-serving interpretation. But most evangelical Christians, women as well as men, genuinely have difficulty in seeing how the objectives of the women's movement can be accommodated to what is taught in Scripture.

The most "liberal" approach to the Scriptural evidence is to claim that even though the New Testament writers may have believed they were reporting God's will when they issued their prohibitions and demands about women, they were really the victims of their own cultural bias, and were simply wrong about what God wanted for Christian women.

But many evangelical Christians are not happy with such dismissal of the Biblical injunctions. They wish to maintain Scripture as God's infallible word (in whatever sense they use that term) and to say that the writers of New Testament epistles were mistaken about something so fundamental as the relationship between the sexes is contrary to their view of Scripture.

Such Christians are often suspicious of any attempts to "interpret" texts in ways that seem to explain away what they take to be the "clear meaning" of the texts. I would like to point out that everyone who reads Scripture must do some interpreting. Taken in context, both in the context of their place in the chapters in which they appear and in their context as statements made to specific people in specific times and places, the texts often quoted as cornerstone references for the place of women in the church, home, and world do not support the conservative or evangelical churches' stance toward women.

My first point is best illustrated by two famous passages from Paul's first letter to the Corinthians. The first is the passage about head coverings in chapter 11, verses 4 through 6. None of the evangelical churches take literally this statement about women praying only with veils or with their heads covered. All have interpreted that passage to be a cultural prohibition relevant only to the time in which it was written.

Then there is the passage in II Corinthians, chapter 14 (v. 34, 35) about women keeping silent in the churches. Again, no church takes this completely literally. If they did, there would be no women in the church choirs, certainly no soloists, no women missionaries giving testimonies or praying. Furthermore, this passage appears at most literal reading to contradict chapter 11 where Paul said that women must have their heads covered when they prophesy. It is difficult to imagine how women could prophesy if they were to be silent. The New English Bible translation of chapter 14 avoids the problem of women singing; its translation is "women should not address the meeting," but it still leaves the problem of how to explain the possibility of their prophesying without "addressing the meeting." In short, there is no such thing as simply taking these passages at their most literal meaning; they cannot be understood without interpretation of some sort, interpretation that involves looking at the context.

Granted then, that every Christian must pay attention to the context in which such texts occur and must attempt to arrive at an interpretation that is consistent with all of Scripture, let us look at the passages that have been most often used in the discussions of women's roles.

1. Creation: Male and Female

Genesis 1:27, 28: "So God created man in his own image; in the image of God he created him; male and female he created them. God blessed them and said to them, 'Be fruitful and increase, fill the earth and subdue it, rule over it'" (NEB). Here there is no distinction made in the status of male and female. They appear to be equals; the command to subdue the earth is given to both; there is no talk of one being a helper to the other. They are together the image of God and are together to rule over the earth.

In the account of Genesis 2, God creates man from the dust of the earth, places him in the garden "to till it and care for it," and gives him the command not to eat of the tree "of the knowledge of good and evil." Then God says, "It is not good for man to be alone. I will provide a partner for him," and God proceeds to form each of the animals from the dust of the ground and bring them to man to see what he will call them, "but for man himself no partner had yet been found." Then God takes the rib from Adam, makes it a woman and brings her to Adam, who says, "Now this, at last—bone of my bone—flesh of my flesh!—this shall be called woman. . . ." The writer of Genesis adds, "That is why man leaves his father and mother and is united to his wife, and the two become one flesh." There is no talk here of subordination. Apparently Eve is an adequate partner for Adam, because she is of his flesh. Note that if Eve's coming from Adam's rib rather than being formed directly by God suggests some subordinate quality, it follows that the animals are on Adam's level because both were made from the dust of the earth. The point here is that husband and wife are to be taken as being *one flesh* in the way that Adam and Eve were one flesh.

Sometimes Adam's prior creation is taken to indicate that women should be quiet and submissive. But the animals, too, were created before Eve, and nobody seriously maintains that women ought to subjugate themselves to animals. Furthermore, one might turn that argument around and point to the climactic order of creation in Genesis 1, and then argue that Eve was loftier than Adam. At any rate, the evidence in Genesis certainly gives no indication that Eve's later creation made her inferior; quite the opposite, it suggests that Adam was incomplete without her and that the two of them, equal and together, were the crown of creation.

The Hebrew word translated *partner* in the NEB (KJ *help meet for*) is used nineteen times in the Old Testament, fifteen times to indicate God's help, and three times to indicate man's (Isa. 30:5 — "no help they find"), conveying each of these three times the idea that man's help is ineffectual. In other words, the Hebrew word does not indicate the kind of subordinate helper we so often take it to mean, somebody who runs errands and tends to the details of living. Rather, the word expresses the kind of helper that God is: a strength to rely on, a constant support, someone who loves and stands with us in trouble and joy.

Paul's statement that "Woman was made for man" is often taken to mean that woman is not to exist in her own right, but only to support man. According to the Hebrew word translated "help" or "helper," one could better put the matter, "Woman was made for man to rely on," which carries the connotation that women are at least as strong and competent as men.

Genesis 3 gives the account of the fall. The woman encounters the serpent, eats the fruit, and "she also gave her husband some and he ate it." Some have seen this as an example of the dreadful consequences if a woman does not consult her husband, but there is no evidence in the text to show that Eve's sin was her failure to consult Adam. "What is this you have done?" says the Lord; and

Eve replies, "The serpent tricked me and I ate." No talk here about "I didn't consult the man you gave me to," but simply "I ate."

Now God pronounces the curse on the serpent, the woman, and the man. The curse to the woman is, "I will increase your labor and your groaning, and in labor you shall bear children. You shall be eager for your husband, and he shall be your master." Is the Hebrew word translated "shall" to be taken as a mere prediction or is it a statement of what *must* be? Most people understand the first "shall" as a prediction. There are few who think that it is immoral to administer anesthetics during childbirth to alleviate the pain. Why, then, is it maintained that the second part of the curse must be a rule—that the husband must be the wife's master?

Plows and electricity and air conditioning have been hailed as manifestations of God's grace in providing relief from the consequences of the curse on man. Is it not possible that the advent of women's rights is equally God's grace in giving them relief from the curse on woman?

The relationship between men and women that existed as a result of the fall into sin was not a healthy one. It was distorted from what God had originally intended marriage to be. Many have declared that because of sin an authority had to be set up in marriage, a superior-inferior relationship that would not have been necessary had man not fallen into sin. However, Christ came to restore all such distorted and broken relationships. If the authority of the man in the marriage is a result of sin, then surely Christian husbands and wives should be working to get rid of that distortion, to return their marriages to the relationship that God originally intended for them, that of equality and partnership in the work God gives them to do.

Evangelical churches frequently interpret Genesis 1 to mean that they must maintain the differences between men and women. Because man was created "male and female" goes this interpretation, clearly there are differences God wishes to maintain. Some churches spell out the differences in terms of a woman being gentler or being a homemaker; others seem to find the chief difference that of women being forbidden leadership roles in the church. But why are Christians so insistent on the differences between the sexes? Genesis 1 speaks of male and female being equally the image of God. To continue to emphasize differences almost suggests that one must be both male and female to be complete or to be fully the human being that God intended. Genesis 1 gives no indication at all that there must be differences between the sexes, or that the sexes must play different roles. Except for the anatomical differences that permit man and woman to become one flesh, and the obvious fact that women will bear the children, there are no other differences between them suggested or stated. It seems to me that Christians are going beyond the Biblical evidence and inserting their own culturally determined beliefs into the text when they insist that there are differences between men and women that must be maintained.

2. The Gospels

The actions of Jesus recorded in the gospels are often cited in discussions of women's roles. In a society that gave women very little respect, where the orthodox Jewish male thanked God every morning that he had not been made a woman, Jesus was remarkable for His attention to women. He spoke to the Samaritan woman, for example, an action just as noteworthy for the fact of a Jewish teacher speaking publicly to a woman as for the fact of a Jew addressing a Samaritan. He told Martha that Mary was following the "better" way, in sitting listening to Him rather than doing her house chores. He refused to condemn the woman taken in adultery. Some have maintained that His most telling defense of women occurred when He let the woman with the issue of blood touch Him and then made a public scene about it. The woman, it is argued, obviously had some kind of menstrual problem. She would be considered unclean, as women were during their menstrual periods. By making a public issue of her touching Him and yet not considering Himself unclean as a result, Jesus was telling His audience that He did not take seriously those Jewish prohibitions about women.

Another case often cited is that Jesus sent Mary to tell His disciples that He had risen from the dead. It was unlawful for a woman to bear witness in a court of law in Israel because her testimony was considered unreliable. By appearing first to Mary and by suggesting that He considered her a reliable witness, Christ was once again showing that He considered women to be equal to men.

The Gospels do not record any incidents in which Jesus acted as if women were inferior persons or as if they ought to have been at home rather than following and listening to Him. To us, this seems perfectly normal behavior. But in a culture in which women were not often allowed public roles and in which even speaking to a woman in public was of doubtful respectability, Jesus' behavior was quite out of the ordinary.

People who wish to insist that women are "equal but different" will point to the fact that Jesus did not appoint any women as disciples. Of course women could not have been disciples in that day, traveling about in mixed company, going on the teaching trips on which Jesus sent His disciples, without being considered loose and immoral women. But Jesus did *all He could in that time and place* to establish the equality of women.

We have no concrete evidence on either side to know whether Jesus would have made women disciples had He come in a different age, or whether He would have insisted that such authoritative roles were only for men. We do have a clear indication that He did not consider women to be inferior in any way and that, contrary to the rabbinical law that women were not allowed to study the Scriptures, He encouraged women to learn about Him and His teachings.

3. The Epistles

Establishing the equality of women with men does not solve the problems, however. For many have maintained that although women are equal, they are different. As women, they are assigned to certain roles, and to only those roles, by God's design. The texts cited for this belief, aside from Genesis 1 and 2, are nearly all taken from the New Testament epistles, mainly Paul's writings.

These texts fall into three different categories or deal with three separate questions: the role of women in the church; the relationship of a married woman to her husband, especially in the matter of authority; and the legitimacy of a career outside the home for a married woman. These three questions must be kept separate. Too often in the past the authority of the husband in the home has been used as evidence that any man automatically holds authority over any woman in any given area, and that female authority is wrong everywhere, even in business, professional, or political life. In the same way, the texts about the place of women in the church are extended to all areas of life, so that decrees such as "women must keep silence in the churches" are taken to indicate that quiet listening is always the appropriate behavior for a Christian woman.

What do these texts from the epistles tell us about the roles the writers of the New Testament expected women to play?

As I mentioned earlier, there are really three separate questions to be dealt with in discussing the Biblical view of women: what role should women play in the church? what is the proper relationship between a Christian husband and wife? and is the only role for women that of wife and mother? Both Genesis 1 and Jesus' attitude toward women clearly establish the fact that women are

45

equal to men in God's eyes. But equality does not answer the question of roles. What does the Bible say about them? What do the epistles tell us about the roles women were to play?

Women in the church

"Is it fitting for a woman to pray to God bareheaded?" Paul asks in I Corinthians 11:13. If we are honest, we are obliged to reply, "Perhaps not in Corinth in the first century, but in America in the twentieth century, yes." Almost all churches have long since decided, quite rightly, that this is a cultural prohibition, not a decree of God laid down for all time. The phrase "Is it fitting?" is particularly important here, for very often Paul's concern is with decorum, with the impression the woman will make on others. Always he wants that impression to be one of modesty and propriety: never is a Christian woman to engage in conduct or appearance that is not "fitting."

In I Corinthians 14, Paul takes up the matter of conducting meetings in good order. "Women should not address the meeting. . . . If there is something they want to know, they can ask their own husbands at home. It is a shocking thing that a woman should address the congregation." Note Paul's reason for the rule: it would be "shocking" for a woman to speak. Once again his concern is for decorum, for doing what is fitting, for "good order" in the worship service. No doubt a woman's speaking publicly would have been shocking in first-century Corinth; respectable women did not speak publicly even to their own husbands. But there would be nothing shocking about hearing a woman speak in the twentieth-century church. In fact, if the church is concerned about its image among unbelievers, which was part of Paul's concern in this chapter (see v. 22), it had much better allow women to speak, since it is shocking to most twentieth-century Americans that the church discriminates so blatantly against women.

Notice, too, that Paul is clearly referring only to married women here (since he says they can go home and ask their husbands). The

46

single woman, the woman who lives alone, was not common in that society. The church will have to decide the role of such women on its own, since the New Testament writers never thought to talk about it.

In I Timothy 3, Paul once again discusses good order in the churches, this time in terms of what kind of men should be office holders. Let us dispose immediately of the argument that because Paul speaks of deacons and elders as being "faithful to one wife" we have evidence that he would not have approved of women holding office in the church. What it in fact shows is that the question never occurred to him. With few exceptions, women were not trained and did not perform public kinds of actions. Naturally if one looked for someone with "a good reputation with the non-Christian public" or someone with a "firm hold on the deep truths of the faith" (the qualifications Paul lays down), one would most readily find these among the men who were experienced in public life and educated. When Paul thought "capable leadership," he thought "men," quite possibly not because there was anything wrong with women assuming leadership but simply because so few women would have been capable. Romans 16:1, in fact, suggests, though the matter is ambiguous, that Phoebe held an office of some kind in the church at Cenchreae.

The final word on women's place in the church occurs in I Timothy 2:9-15. "I do not permit a woman to be a teacher, nor must woman domineer over man; she should be quiet." The Greek word translated "woman" here, as in the other passages, can equally well mean "married woman" and the Greek word for "man," "husband." The Dutch Reformed theologian N. J. Hommes insists that the "teaching" in this passage refers to a kind of admonishing that does not occur in our churches. What Paul was concerned with, he says, is that a woman not admonish her husband publicly (*Calvin Theological Journal,* April, 1969, pp. 5-22).

This stance fits in very well with one explanation of the apparent contradiction between I Corinthians 11 and 14. In chapter 11,

47

goes this explanation, Paul is talking about a service attended only by committed Christians. Shortly after he finishes his discussion about women keeping their heads covered to pray and prophesy, he criticizes the behavior of Corinthians when they "meet as a congregation," especially to take the Lord's Supper. It is explained that this kind of meeting was a meeting where there were no unbelievers present. At such meetings women were allowed to speak.

In I Corinthians 14, on the other hand, Paul is discussing public meetings, meetings at which unbelievers might be present (see v. 22). In such meetings women should not address the congregation —or ask questions, as the context suggests—because it is a shocking thing. They should keep their place "as the law directs," not because Christians had to live by that old law, but because in the presence of those who were not Christians, Christian women's behavior should not be such as to bring disrepute on the church.

If we accept this explanation of two kinds of meetings the passage in Timothy is clearer. Allowing women to question publicly or to admonish in such meetings would appear to be letting them domineer over their husbands. Timothy's injunction has nothing to do with the function of ruling the church or being active in benevolence, or even with the kind of preaching that occurs in our churches where we do not have the personal questioning and admonishing that is suggested here.

A difficulty in interpreting this text lies in the Greek word translated "domineer over." This is the only time that word is used in the entire New Testament. It is related to the word for *master* or *autocrat,* and therefore might quite properly be translated "be the master over." Whether having some kind of official authority in the church would automatically make a woman domineer over her husband is debatable. It seems quite possible that there is a sense of "domineer over" that has nothing to do with official positions of leadership, but rather refers to a relationship between people that might be unhealthy even if the man were doing the domineering.

In view of the concern Paul has that female behavior be decorous or fitting, it seems clear that his prohibitions concerning women are directed to a specific time and place. Further, the abiding truth of the underlying principle—that women, like all Christians, should behave decorously and not offensively, especially in the worship service—does not indicate that in twentieth-century North America a woman ought not to speak publicly or hold an office in the church.

Occasionally those insisting that women may not hold authority in the church will argue the case from the "headship" of man. But in every case where that headship is asserted, it is in a description of the marriage relationship, not a description of church order.

Husbands and wives

The question of a married woman's relationship to her husband is quite a different matter from the problem of woman's role in the church, and the two questions ought to be kept distinct. Because they are not, however, unmarried women and widows are left almost totally outside some churches' authority structures. Those women are expected to support themselves and to contribute to the church budget, just as working men do, but the women are not allowed to have the same voice in church affairs that men have. (Married women can at least try to influence their husbands.) In all of his discussions about women in the church Paul is speaking of married women; the position of unmarried women, independent and financially equal to men, is simply not dealt with.

What then of a married woman's relationship to her husband? She is to "be subject to him" (Eph. 5:22 and Col. 3:18, among others), for "the man is head of the woman as Christ also is head of the church" (Eph. 5:22, 23). An interesting point about the Ephesians passage is that the verse immediately preceding the one about wives says, referring to the relationship of all Christians to one another, "Be subject to one another." The Greek here is sometimes translated "obey," sometimes "be in submission to," but whatever we take it to mean, the point is that a woman's relationship to her husband's authority is very much like the relationship of all Christians to one another.

The picture of the marriage relationship presented in these passages is a beautiful one. It is by no means the traditional one of the woman saying "yes, dear" to the man (and frequently conniving to get her own way anyhow). The picture is of two fully adult human beings, encouraging each other in whatever their work in the kingdom may be. The woman consults her husband, listens to his advice, seriously considers his words—*just as all Christians should of one another.*

The Ephesians passage continues "for man is head of the woman just as Christ also is the head of the church." This passage suggests some way in which a man is the representative or authority or official in the family, but the exact way is not very clear.

For one thing, the writers of the New Testament did not have an understanding of the central nervous system and the fact that all our actions are controlled or "ordered" by our brain or head. To their way of thinking, the ordering or thinking part of man was the heart, not the head. Hence, whatever headship means, it does *not* mean the right to give orders or have total authority over every aspect of family life.

Headship today sometimes takes on the meaning of "first among equals" such as the head of a department in an organization, or the way the chairman may be said to head-up a committee. Sometimes headship is given simply to the first-born, as in societies where the "head" of the family is the eldest son. He has certain responsibilities as well as certain privileges as a result. The concept of headship as applied to the marriage relationship certainly needs more analysis by Christians genuinely interested in exploring the meaning of the concept in a world where the woman in the family may be independently wealthy, more knowledgeable than her husband, better equipped to make decisions, more reliable—and in any number of other ways better prepared to be the decision-making member of the family.

It is possible, of course, for headship to be only a representative function. The man of the house might represent the family legally (a practice indicated by the wife's taking the husband's name, for example), but most evangelical Christians think that the concept has more content than that.

Let us explore for a bit that metaphor of *headship* as it applies to Christ as head of the church. Almost none of the roles and duties assigned to women follow from this metaphor. Christ's headship of the church does not suggest that all church members must do the same kind of work, nor does the headship of man suggest that all women must be homemakers. Christ's headship does not suggest that the church must be protected from dangers and difficulties, nor do women need protection from difficult work. Christ's headship does not imply that the church may make no decisions for itself, or that it should be cloistered, or that it should devote itself mainly to serving Christ's needs. In the same way, the man's headship of the family does not imply that women may not be decision-makers, or that they should not get out into the wicked world, or that they should devote themselves chiefly to serving their husband's personal needs.

In short, whatever the man's headship of the family implies, it does not imply that a woman may not have a career, nor that his career must take precedence over hers, nor that the man must be the sole support of his family, nor that a woman must keep house, nor that she must devote herself to caring for the man's personal needs, nor that all decision-making resides in the man.

Christ demands that the church use every ounce of her talent and strength in advancing the kingdom; that she go out dynamically into the world, working and praying mightily; that she develop and grow as much as possible so that there may be greater maturity and ability available for the kingdom's work. How many men expect that of their wives?

51

Still another possible interpretation of male authority arises from Paul's injunctions for slaves to obey their masters. Christianity was not intended to work a revolution in social matters (or was intended to do so only insofar as people who became Christians might begin treating other people in revolutionary ways). Hence, Paul did not abolish slavery but merely suggested that if slaves and masters treated each other as Christians should treat other people, there would be little difficulty. Perhaps the injunctions about male authority were intended much the same way, not as statements that men *ought* to be in authority, but simply as statements to the effect that women ought, like slaves, not upset the social applecart by refusing an attitude toward their husbands that society demanded of them.

Some Christians feel that the analogy of Christ's headship of the church makes that interpretation impossible, but others feel that just as Christ's headship of the church does not impose specific forms or regulations on the church, so the male headship of the family does not impose any specific restrictions on the structure of the marriage relationship.

Some of the texts concerning women are really very difficult to interpret, but those difficulties are often shoved aside and the part of the text that emphasizes women's submission is exaggerated. First Timothy 2:15 says, "She shall be saved through motherhood," a text that on its most literal interpretation clearly contradicts the teaching of salvation through faith alone. "A woman must be a learner, listening quietly," even though we now know that learning is not best served by "listening quietly," but by the freedom to ask questions and pursue difficulties. "And it was not Adam who was deceived; it was the woman, yielding to deception fell into sin." But surely Adam also was deceived, for if he was not deceived, he deliberately *chose* damnation with Eve over devotion to God, a choice less commendable than a mistake made through being deceived. This text is difficult to interpret in several ways. It is neither good exegesis, nor fair practice, I think, to pick out bits and

52

pieces of it to apply to women when clearly we do not understand it in its entirety.

Careers

No conflict exists between any of the above passages and careers for married women. A woman could be president of General Motors and still fulfil all of the admonitions about her relationship to her husband. Only one text in the Bible can be taken to enforce the notion that woman's place is *only* at home. Titus 2:3-5 reads, "The older women should be reverent in their bearing, not scandal-mongers or slaves to strong drink; they must set a high standard and school the younger women to be loving wives and mothers, temperate, chaste, and kind, busy at home. . . ." All of these virtues we should certainly encourage in wives, and career-minded Christian wives and mothers would have no objection to them. The question is whether *busy at home* is intended to set the limits of the woman's function. I cannot believe that given this context—of not being scandal-mongers or slaves to strong drink—Paul intended anything here but that women should be busy in their work rather than sitting about gossiping. For Paul, women's work was in the home, simply as a cultural fact. If we take this passage to be a prohibition on women's working outside the home, we must explain Lydia, who was a seller of purple (though we don't know that she was married), and the ideal wife of Proverbs 31:

> After careful thought she buys a field
> and plants a vineyard with her earnings. . . .
> She sees that her business goes well. . . .
> She weaves linen and sells it,
> and supplies merchants with their sashes.

This passage from Proverbs, traditionally used to show how women must busy themselves in work at home, indicates clearly something that we shall discuss more fully in chapter three. Women's work in previous ages was not limited to the care of

53

small children and the cleaning of a six-room house. The house-wife of Proverbs 31 had challenging work to do, work that in our day has been taken over by men: grape growing, buying and selling real estate, weaving cloth, and selling clothing. One cause of the women's movement is precisely this fact of the ever-decreasing work-load of housewives.

What, then, is the answer to our three questions? The passages on women's role *in the church* are constantly reiterating the theme of decorum, so that the church would not become a place of impropriety or scandal, and would not be offensive to non-Christians in the community. Surely such a principle should not prohibit women from taking leadership roles in the twentieth century.

The passages on *marriage* do indicate an authority of some kind on the part of the male. What, precisely, the content of the authority is in the twentieth century needs to be explored much more fully. But whatever its content, the relationship suggested is one that would bring about growth, maturity, and creative development for both marriage partners, not one which would keep women "in their place."

There is simply no Biblical evidence at all to suggest that woman's place is *at home*. Even if she were required to obey her husband in the most abject meaning of *obey*, even if she were never to open her mouth in church, even if she were saved by bearing children, none of that in any way suggests that she is forbidden to have a career outside the home.

4. Equality

The Biblical evidence for women's full equality with men has been a long problem for theologians. The clearest statement of equality is Galatians 3:28: "There is no such thing as Jew and Greek . . . male and female; for you are all one person in Christ Jesus." Theologians have spent much time and ingenuity attempting to show that men and women can be equal in Christ—and in Christ's body, the church—and at the same time women can be denied the right to leadership. But no matter how one labors over words and definitions, "equality" that systematically denies leadership roles to some of those with ability is simply not equality. Suppose some church were to declare that although races are obviously equal (no such thing as Jew and Greek) nonetheless members of one of the races should not be allowed to hold office in that church. Nobody would be fooled into believing that such a church really believed in equality for the races. So, too, for all the theologians' struggles to make it compatible, this text simply cannot be reconciled with a refusal to let women exercise the same leadership as men.

Since they cannot be reconciled, one is left with a choice of two views: either the New Testament prohibitions and rules are culturally influenced and full equality is the eternal will of God, or the rules and prohibitions are the eternal will of God and this statement of equality is in some way culturally bound or mistaken or mistranslated or whatever. In view of the cultural situation of the day, and Paul's constant emphasis on decorum as the reason for his rules, surely the former is the more likely explanation.

Finally, the attitude of some churches toward unmarried women has long been one of blatant discrimination and injustice. Women are allowed in some evangelical churches to teach theology on the mission field, but not to preach a sermon at home. Women are some of the most dedicated and talented mission workers the churches have, yet women are often forbidden the right to membership on the boards and committees that decide mission policy. They are expected to support themselves, and the church, but are not allowed any voice in how the church spends the money they give it. They are totally without representation in the official organization of many churches. In the society of the New Testament writers, unmarried women were given support and protection by some man—father, husband, brother—somebody took legal, moral, and financial responsibility for them. Any church that denies to unmarried women that support, yet at the same time forbids them equal rights, is clearly guilty of injustice.

CHAPTER
THREE

Where Does a Christian Stand?

In any movement intent on bringing change to a society, the adherents tend to go to extremes about some things in order to counter what they consider to be extremes in the status quo. This is true of the women's movement. In an attempt to find freedom for women, the advocates sometimes neglect to point out women's responsibilities. In their desire to make clear the detrimental effects of sex discrimination among women, the feminists often forget or dismiss the detrimental effects of sex discrimination on men. Above all, in declaring that woman's status in the family is responsible for many of what they consider to be the evils of her position, they tend to dismiss the family as an unnecessary, or even a harmful, institution.

Christians should not fall victim to any of these unbalanced views. In analyzing and evaluating the women's movement, Christians must keep firmly in mind the responsibilities of marriage partners to each other, and to their children; the importance of service to other people in the Christian scheme of life; and the value of a strong family unit in preparing children for mature, responsible adulthood.

But there are many goals in the women's movement that should be considered by Christians. Some of these objectives are not matters that can be settled only by reference to Christian principles. The question of what constitutes adequate day care, for example, needs to be settled partially by looking at the effects of day care on children, not by reference to what was done in Bible times. The question of whether or not the state should pay for day care is also not a question to be settled by reference only to Christian principles, but should include an awareness of the kind of state the people of a certain nation choose to live in. So it is with some other questions raised by the feminists.

There are five areas, I think, in which the objectives of the women's movement call for Christian analysis, areas in which Christian principles clearly indicate the response Christians should make. Those areas are abortion, family life, the use of women's talents, the marriage relationship, and sexual attitudes.

1. Abortion

The first disagreement a Christian must have with the women's movement is on the issue of abortion. The point at issue in the debate is whether the fetus is or is not a human being with all the rights that we grant to human beings. If the fetus is considered human, certain obligations toward it follow. If the fetus is considered a piece of tissue or a form of subhuman life, most of those obligations disappear. Most feminists insist, when they debate the issue of the fetus' humanity at all, that since we do not know that it is a human being, we are entitled to consider it as something less. Christians must, I think, declare otherwise: since it *might* be a human being, we must be cautious and refuse to destroy it without the kind of reasons that might, in other circumstances, justify destroying human life. To borrow an analogy, would one fire a revolver into a closet that *might* hold a human being?

The most common argument used by the feminists, that a woman has a right to her own body and therefore has a right to decide if she will carry a baby to birth, is based on the assumption that the fetus is not human. Human beings have rights to their own bodies only when no other human bodies might be affected. We require people to have vaccinations, for example, as much to protect other members of the community as to protect the vaccinated members. We quarantine people if we think their being at large might be a danger to the rest of the populace. People do not have an un-limited right to control of their own bodies. If the fetus is not a human being but a subhuman form of life, of course, removing it at the woman's discretion is much like removing any other "para-site" that she does not wish to have around. But if the fetus is human, or even if it might be human, then the woman's right to control of her body is limited by the other human's (the fetus') right to its body.

All of the feminist arguments about abortion assume something about human sexuality that Christians ought not accept. The feminists assume that engaging in sexual intercourse should be an act that is free to any adults who wish to do so, and that the female adult should not have to bear the consequences of possible pregnancy unless she wants to. The Christian's positions on responsibility and adultery make the Christian take a different view of this matter. There may, of course, be cases where pregnancy is the result of force or of ignorance, but if knowledgeable adults choose to engage in sexual intercourse, they must be willing to bear the consequences of that action. They may not avoid those consequences by lightly taking another life.

In discussing abortion the feminists do make some good points. Those who control medical research in this country seem not to care whether or not they find a safe contraceptive that has no side effects. The desire for such a contraceptive is obvious. Millions of women continue to take contraceptive pills even when they know the pills may be harmful, or when the pills produce irritating or dangerous side effects. And the women who do this are not promiscuous, unmarried career women; they are mostly married women who already have some children. The people doing research on contraceptives are employees of drug companies. There is no government funding, no public effort of any size to meet this need that is important to so many citizens. Feminists are quite sure that this unconcern is an example of male refusal to take seriously the needs of women. Whatever its cause, the situation should surely be remedied.

Still another point in the abortion debate must be taken seriously by Christians. If we are to require women to bear children they do not want to raise, if we are to require young girls, many of whom become pregnant out of sheer ignorance, to bear their babies, we must offer places for them to go, and counseling and understanding to see them through this difficult period. It is un-Christian, if not unjust, to tell a sixteen-year-old that she must carry her baby to term, and then not offer her a home to stay in while she is pregnant, a place to have the baby where she will not be embarrassed, expert counseling to help her understand herself, and so on.

It is equally un-Christian to decree that married women must bear children they do not want, and then offer them no help in raising those children. If a couple has financial problems or emotional problems or problems of genetic origin and we offer no support or help to them, we ought not sit in judgment on the couple's decision to abort a pregnancy. Only if we stand ready to help, to share the burden, may we advise or insist that the couple be willing to accept another child.

Sadly enough, the atmosphere of many Christian communities is so judgmental, so critical of any sexual deviation that women in those communities are driven to seek abortions. If we take seriously the woman's obligation to continue the life growing within her, we must also take seriously our obligation to accept her in love and understanding, no matter what she has done.

A further point must be made. Many state laws require a woman to submit to her husband's desire for intercourse. In many states, a marriage may be annulled if it has not been physically consummated, and refusal to grant a man his "conjugal rights" is grounds for divorce in others. Until we have a reliable contraceptive that all women can use, such laws virtually require a woman to bear children if her *husband* wants them. Those laws are unjust and should be changed.

Whether or not a Christian believes in abortion in cases of rape, incest, and such things will depend upon how literally he takes the command not to kill. Some Christians will argue that abortion is not justified even to save the mother's life while others feel that there are conditions under which an only-potential human life may be sacrificed for the health or well-being of a fully developed human life. Whatever position a Christian holds on these points, all Christians must, I think, object to the demand for abortion for anyone who wants it for whatever reason. Human life cannot be treated so cavalierly by anyone who considers it a gift from God.

2. Family Life

Opponents of the women's movement can cite story after story of women who have left their families to go seeking their own identities, women who have denied their obligations to their families because they wanted to become free spirits. It is true that many women use the doctrines of feminism to justify such behavior. And it is also true that some leaders of the movement think such behavior justified if a woman finds herself in a situation that prevents her from finding satisfaction. Those feminists do not take seriously enough the commitment to marriage or to raising children that women make when they become wives and mothers.

Even some Christian women have fallen victim to the idea that fulfilling their own needs or desires is justification for any behavior they find satisfactory. Christians interested in feminism must insist that such attitudes are wrong. Responsibilities cannot be ignored or wiped out when the person who has assumed them becomes unhappy or bored with her situation. She must rather continue to carry those responsibilities while she works to change or improve her situation.

Particularly in the area of divorce, Christians must part ways with most feminists. Even the most radical feminists grant that a woman has *some* obligations to her children, but many of them feel there is no obligation at all to permanency in marriage. They believe that if the marriage is not meeting one's needs or desires, it should be terminated. Whether Christians believe there are never grounds for divorce, or they accept some grounds in some situations, Christians can never accept the attitude that marriage is an on-again, off-again proposition based entirely on how people feel about holding it together. Along with the demand for responsible sexual behavior, Christian feminists must insist on permanency in marriage.

Authority

Precisely because they believe in permanent marriage, many Christians worry about feminism's challenge to male authority. They believe that if we begin to tamper with the traditional authority in the family, the family will be left with no authority at all. If there is no agreed-upon method of settling an impasse, goes this argument, the only alternative is divorce. Therefore if we believe in the permanency of marriage, we must also believe in the authority of the man.

In those few and far-between cases where a husband and wife come to a complete impasse in their ability to settle something, it is probably true that there must be some agreed-upon authority. But how often do such impasses occur? I have never had a single one in fifteen years of married life. When two people are supposedly living together in love, one would expect that the refusal of either to grant that the other might have a point is an indication that something more than a question of authority is involved. If two people cannot come to some compromise, or cannot agree to submit an issue to arbitration by some third party, they probably are not fighting over the issue, but over some emotional need or an under-the-surface issue.

Let us grant, however, that such impasses may occur. In such cases it probably is wise to have authority automatically at hand. Theoretically, this view would allow authority to rest with either the man or the woman, but since the traditional way is for the male to have that authority, there is no reason to change.

The position that one of the two people in a marriage must be the authority often takes the form of claiming that there had to be a leader and God chose the man for that role. The false assumption made in such a statement is that there "has to be a leader." In spite

66

of what people claim, most marriages actually operate on a system of divided authority. In some, usually rather haphazard, way the couple comes to agreement about who is responsible for what; from then on authority in a given area rests with that partner. He may have total and unquestioned authority over all matters pertaining to the car, for example, while she has complete authority over the best methods of baby care. In some major areas there may be no clear authority; such matters must be discussed and, if there is disagreement, compromises reached.

People intent on proving the male authority in a home will insist that any authority vested in the woman is only delegated authority from the man. But let such a man tell his wife what to serve for dinner, or how many times a day to feed the baby, or how to arrange her time, or which detergent to use, and it will soon become clear that there are *some* areas where her authority is absolute. We are carrying on a charade when we say men have, or ought to have, authority in every area of homelife. If we mean by male authority only that in a rock-bottom disagreement, his vote counts more than hers, it is probably sensible to have such an arrangement. I doubt that it will be used more than two or three times in a lifetime.

Structure

Another fear that Christians have about feminism is that the changes in family structure advocated by the feminists are attempts to tamper with what is God-ordained, or with a structure that has worked well for thousands of years, or with what is "natural."

There is little evidence for maintaining that the *current structure* of the family is God-ordained. Christians must stoutly insist against all doubters, including the radical feminists, that the family is God's chosen instrument for the nurture of children. But the present American family is not the same structure that existed in even the recent past, much less the same as that of Biblical times.

The separation of the nuclear family (father, mother, and children) into separate living units, isolated from and independent of the extended family (aunts, uncles, grandparents, cousins), is a twentieth-century phenomenon that no Biblical writer foresaw. When people in past times spoke of "family" they did not mean a unit of two adults with one to five children; they meant something closer to what we would call a clan.

Another contemporary phenomenon that makes family life quite different today from what it was in the past is the development of schools. The fact that children are taken out of the home many hours a day makes family life and motherhood an entirely different thing from what it used to be. Add to that the increasing ease of housekeeping and the distance of the father's work from the home, and you have a situation that in almost no respect resembles that of even a hundred years ago.

These changes are the direct cause of the frustration that makes women join the liberation movement. The confinement to a home where there are no other adults, the ease and consequent boringness of most housework, the disappearance of children for most of the day and the fact that their children's lives tend to center on the school—these are precisely the factors that cause women to find homemaking less rewarding than it may have been in previous years.

We can hardly claim, taking into account the changing family structure, that the feminists' desire to change the American family is an attempt to change a God-ordained structure. Those who advocate the *destruction* of the family must, of course, be resisted. But those who want *changes* in roles are only adapting to changes in family life that have already occurred.

The position that the family has served society for thousands of years is vulnerable to the same arguments given above. The contemporary family simply is *not* the structure that survived all those years. Furthermore, the American family is no longer working successfully, and the blame does not lie with the feminists. The breakdown of American family life began at least as far back as the Second World War, quite probably, further back, with the rise of industrialization. The current wave of feminism did not begin until 1963, when the American family was already far along the road to disaster. Feminists are not tampering with a successful venture when they urge changes in family life; they are rather advocating modifications that may well strengthen a deteriorating structure.

Child care

Some Christians argue that it is "natural" for women to stay home with children, that women are more patient, or more gentle, or more passive, or in some other way endowed by nature with the ability to handle youngsters and create a home.

Except for certain anatomical and physiological differences, we simply do not know what men and women are by nature. We cannot say for certain that men and women differ by nature on any point because we have no control group that has not been conditioned by the society in which they grew up. It may be that it is impossible to have such a group, that without conditioning into certain attitudes and roles human beings cannot develop at all. Be that as it may, the fact is that we do not know, on either scientific or Biblical grounds, what differences between the sexes exist *by nature*.

The fact that most societies have allowed dominance to men is often cited as evidence that such a way is the "natural" way for people to live. But the evidence is not conclusive. It is just as likely that man's sheer physical strength was misused to assert his dominance over the weaker women as that his dominance was "natural." Just as the strong have lorded it over the weak in political life, so, it may be, the superior strength of the man was used to keep his woman in line. Surely among Christians such might-makes-right methods should be dismissed.

But let us assume for a moment that there might be broad differences between the two groups. To choose at random some possibilities, let us assume that in fact men are more mechanical, more active, and more aggressive than women. That tells us nothing about how we ought to treat the two groups, or the individuals in those groups. In any large group of people, the variations of character within the group will be just as large as the differences between that group and any other group. In other words, the most "masculine" of the women will be more masculine than the most "feminine" of the men. The most "masculine" women, then, will be more aggressive and mechanical and active than many of the men. Ought they, because they happen to belong to the group "women," be refused jobs and outlets that permit them to use those characteristics? Ought they be looked down upon because they don't happen to fit the majority pattern in their group? Ought the "feminine" men, the ones who are gentle and passive and unmechanical be refused jobs that make use of those characteristics? Of course not. So that, even if women-as-a-group were better prepared to care for small children than men-as-a-group, that tells us nothing about any individual woman or any individual man. It tells us nothing about how such things should be arranged in any individual marriage. It tells us that the proportion of men who choose homemaking may be lower than the proportion of women, but not that any given man should *not* choose homemaking or that any given woman *must* choose homemaking.

Other arguments about women's being by nature mothers and homemakers rest on the premise that a woman's ability to bear and nurse children indicates that she was intended by nature, or by God, to be the parent who cares for the children. A woman's physical make-up surely indicates that she is the parent who is intended to bear and nurse *babies;* nobody can deny that. But that does not indicate that her entire life should be devoted to child care, or that most of the child's life should be lived under the tutelage of the mother.

In the past—even fifty years ago—children were not the sole responsibility of the mother for nine to fourteen hours a day. Once babies could walk, they were as likely to be toddling around after their fathers in the barn or the shop or the store as to be with their mothers.

Furthermore, in grandma's day, there were often relatives or hired girls living in with the family: grandpa's parents, an unmarried uncle, a widowed sister. Somebody was there besides the mother to be answering the children's questions, keeping them out of mischief, showing them how to build bird houses or bake cookies. And father was there. He was there three meals a day, seven days a week. If he wasn't in the house, he was in the barn or the shop. If anyone wanted him, he was available. If mother got tired of children under foot she could shoo them all out to "help" father or she could turn them over to the hired girl for awhile. In short, she did not have the responsibility for raising children that a contemporary mother has. Since father exercised his authority in an immediate hour-to-hour way, it might even be more accurate to say that he raised the children. The statement that it is natural for mothers to raise children or that it has always been done that way is not true.

Many people are against careers for mothers not on the grounds of nature or tradition but on the grounds that children need a parent around many hours a day, that child care arrangements that turn children over to adults outside the family will damage the children. Those who maintain this position would accept the feminist proposals for half-time work for each parent, but would balk at their proposals for day care centers or for professional mothers-helpers.

There is no evidence to indicate that children need their own parents around hours every day to make them grow up emotionally or psychologically healthy. We have long known that children do not need their physical parents, that adoption works well, so that argument is really based on the belief that a child cannot cope with a daily *change* from one adult to another or from one set of adults to another as his authority figure. Yet children have been doing

71

this for centuries. Wealthy parents have never done most of the child care themselves; they have always had diapers changed and toddlers fed by hired help. Nannies, nurses, governesses, even wet nurses, have been raising children for centuries. The children who spent most of their day with their nurse, seeing their parents only perhaps an hour in the morning and several hours in the evening seem to have survived as well as the children of the middle classes who have had their mothers with them all day every day. Even in the middle classes, children were often *cared for* by unmarried aunts and hired girls, even if their mothers were in the house.

It is difficult to convince American middle-class parents that anyone else can be an adequate substitute in caring for their children, yet there is no evidence to support this belief in the necessity of parental presence. The generation of American children brought up by the stay-at-home mothers of the fifties does not seem to be noticeably better adjusted than the generation brought up by the working mothers of the forties. The percentage of mothers in the work force declined noticeably from the forties to the fifties, yet the effect on the children is, so far as one can tell from casual observation, negligible. For every child who suffers a sense of neglect because his mother worked, there is another child who suffers from dependency or rebellion because his mother was too much present in his life. What little evidence we have[1] suggests that a mother's working or not working is not directly correlated with any good or ill effects in the children.

The fact that children do not need a parent with them all day every day must not be taken to indicate that every mother should go out and get a job. Many mothers will still want to be the person who is most important in their children's lives; they will want to be there for every first tooth and first step. While some feminists talk as if they do not approve of anyone making full-time mother-

[1] F. Ivan Nye and Lois Hofman, *The Employed Mother in America* (Rand McNally & Co., 1963).

hood her job, most feminists want only the freedom for women to *choose* what they will do when children arrive in the home. And Christians can, I think, agree with that goal, provided that both parents always keep in mind their responsibility to the children and to each other.

To say that children do not need a parent with them most of the time is not the same as blithely consigning them to group care. Group care, especially for infants, is not the same as a one-to-one relationship with a mother substitute. One of the dangers of the feminist movement is that it too easily assumes that group care will be good for infants when in fact we have almost no evidence about its effects. There is considerable evidence that adequate day care does not damage most children past the age of two, in fact that it may be very healthy for them. The child's welfare must be of prime consideration, and the fact that different children have different needs must be taken into account. The maintenance of day care centers must not become another way in which we victimize children by assuming that what is good for many is good for all.

In the matter of establishing day care centers, Christians should remember that many mothers simply must work, either because they are the heads of their families or because their husbands' jobs are genuinely inadequate to support their families.[2] In such cases the feminist argument that day care is similar to public education is legitimate, I think. Surely it is better for society and for the children that the children be in supervised, professionally-run programs than that they be left with inadequate mother-substitutes or no supervision at all. It is too easy for middle-class people to see day care as a way for mothers to do what they *want;* for many lower-income people, day care is a way for mothers to do what they *must* without damage to the children.

In discussing the care of children Christians are tempted to insist that children must have what is best for them, that children's

2 In 1970, ten million working women were widowed, divorced, or had husbands earning less than $5000 a year. *Discrimination Against Women.*

needs must come ahead of their parents' needs. "One must do what is best for the child," they say very seriously. We ought to face the fact, in discussing child care, that few parents ever do "what is best for the child." Parents can do what is best only within their means and the limits of their own personalities and situations. It may be best for a child of limited intellectual ability to grow up in a home where intellectual ability does not matter, but if it happens that both his parents are highly educated, intellectual people, there is little anyone can do about it. It may be best for a child to attend a private school geared to his particular needs with classes of no more than fifteen students, but if parents do not have the financial means to provide such education, the child will simply have to live with those limitations.

In the same way, the child's needs cannot be made to take precedence over the mother's needs. We must leave room, in discussing child care arrangements, for the realization that mothers, too, have *needs,* that bearing a child does not automatically cancel all of a woman's needs outside of motherhood. Many young mothers are literally unable to survive the regime of twelve hours a day with preschoolers. Too often women have been made to feel, sometimes by the church, that their needs are not really needs but only whims, that if they were less selfish or had more faith, they could be happy doing what they are being required to do. I submit that such a view is false and is damaging to women. Women who find that full-time child care is not fulfilling or satisfying to them should not be made to feel guilty about it; they should realize that women, too, are individuals with differing needs, that just as all men cannot be happy in the same job, so all women cannot be content with full-time motherhood.

Christian parents must, however, do what is best for their children within their own abilities and means. Having brought children into the world, parents are duty-bound to give them what they need.

But it is important to keep in mind the distinction between what children *need* and what they *want*. The fact that children dislike their mother's working does not indicate that they need her presence. Furthermore, what children are thought to need may differ considerably from their actual needs. That a child's *needs* should take precedence over his mother's *desires* is clear; so should they take precedence over his father's desires. But suppose the genuine needs of a parent and child do conflict. Then a compromise will have to be reached in which *each* settles for something less than total fulfillment of his needs. Neither parents' nor children's needs can be ignored without severe consequences to the mental health of the parent or child and the emotional stability of the home.

Ironically, one of the genuine needs of children is ignored by the insistence on full-time motherhood: the need to be given responsibility. For more years than in any other country or culture, American children are allowed to be care-free dependents. They are given freedom without being required to take on corresponding responsibilities. They are given toys without being expected to care for them, they are given cars without being asked to work for them or to use them for the family's benefit. In such ways as helping with the housework, making meals, supervising younger children, doing the family shopping, children, especially adolescents, could be genuinely contributing to the family's functioning. If mothers were not ever-present sources of these services, more of them would become the responsibility of the children.

One thing American children clearly need is more time with their fathers. Feminist goals are designed to produce exactly what Christians should be demanding: that the obligations of fatherhood be taken more seriously. Even in such simple matters as the amount of time they spend at home few Christian men take as seriously their own duty to their children as they take their wives' duties to the children. We have the preacher telling mothers they must stay at home while he himself is not home more than one evening a week. At a recent meeting of Christian parents on how to be better parents a number of the men present admitted that this

Thursday night meeting was their fourth evening that week away from home. We consistently stress the demands of motherhood—so much so that many women feel they are inadequate mothers—while we let fatherhood drift into unimportance.

Typically, men between about twenty-five and fifty are expected to be passionately involved in their work, to be raising their families, and to be carrying the major responsibility for affairs in their communities and churches. Meanwhile, retired men and women have little to occupy them, young men and women (those who are unmarried or who do not yet have families) are expected to assume very few responsibilities, and the wives of the responsible men are confined to their homes with babies or are thought to be incompetent for leadership positions. Surely some better distribution of work can be devised. Christians should be welcoming the feminist demand that women's talents be used, especially when their talents can be used to replace those of men who need to spend more time as fathers.

One last comment on the working mother. When a Christian mother does work her reason is often accepted more readily by other Christians if the reason involves money. "I'm putting John through medical school," or "We just can't make ends meet," or "I'm working to pay for Christian education," or even "for violin lessons." These reasons are more acceptable to fellow Christians than "I'm working because I love my work." Yet Christians have always insisted that work was more than a way to make money; work has intrinsic value as a way of fulfilling man's needs. In the Garden, Adam and Eve were given work to do, and Christians have seen the significance of that. But the values have been reversed for women. Women may work if it is for the money, but not if it is for the sheer love of the job. This is a sad and ironic revelation of our real priorities.

I have so far maintained that there is little evidence to support the belief that the "traditional" family structure of mother at home and father away at work is the best possible one. I have tried to demonstrate that some changes in that structure might be better for the contemporary family and, at the least, that such changes will not be damaging.

The role of the housewife

I would now like to point out that what we call the traditional role of the housewife is not really traditional at all. What the contemporary woman who chooses to be a housewife is choosing is something quite different from what her grandmother had. The label is the same, but the job is quite different.

In grandma's day, families of six to ten children were not uncommon. Grandma had to do all the cooking, baking, canning, and preserving for this brood. She often did most of the sewing involved in keeping them clothed as well. Cleaning meant getting rid of the soot and dust produced by a coal furnace or wood-burning stove. The washing took far longer than it does today—even with fewer clothes—and the ironing was immense. The work involved in merely keeping her family fed was more than a contemporary woman needs to do in the whole process of homemaking.

But the amount of work is not the most essential difference. The important difference between grandma and her granddaughters is that grandma's work was essential to her family. If grandma didn't grow vegetables, can them, bake bread, make pickles, and cook baby food, her family could not survive. The contemporary woman, on the other hand, once her children are in school, can do everything necessary for the survival of the family in three hours a day at the most. Most of her time she spends doing things that are not necessary, no matter how much her family may *like* them. If she decides to hang her sheets outdoors, or to bake her own bread, or to sew her own clothes, or to hang her own wallpaper, or to teach her daughter to cook, or her son astronomy, she does it out of choice, not because her family *needs* her to do those things. Most of what she makes could be purchased (could certainly be purchased if she had a paying job), and most of what she chooses to teach her children, they could learn elsewhere. I am not saying that doing these things has *no value*, note, but only that they are not *essential* to the family's well-being. The contemporary woman has become a purveyor of luxuries, while grandma was a supplier of necessities.

In becoming a luxury, the modern housewife has also become a dependent. Grandma may have been listed as a dependent by the income tax people, but that was only because of the prejudice of the men running the tax department. She was an equal worker with grandpa in the survival of the family; on the farm she was obviously an equal partner and in many family-run city businesses, she was also an essential member of the partnership. That is no longer true. Most of what she spends her time doing is not necessary to the family, and she plays no part at all in the family "business," that is, the means by which the family earns its keep. Again, I am not suggesting that because most of her work is the providing of luxuries, she must stop doing it; I am only saying that it is foolish to insist that her work is of a vital nature when actually *most* of her time is spent on nonessentials. It is precisely that sense of "Why am I doing this?" that makes housework an unsatisfying job for some women.

There is another important difference between grandma and granddaughter. Grandmother quit school in the eighth grade to help out at home. Reading and writing never played a very large part in her life; she had, therefore, little entrance to a world of ideas or to the possibilities for another way of life. My grandmother had eighteen granddaughters: every one of them finished high school. All but four of them had some training beyond high school, nine of them finished college, four have masters' degrees, one is a Ph.D. Granddaughter is not the same person grandma was. It is one thing for a person with rather limited horizons to spend her life providing essential services for her family; it is another thing for a person with much broader horizons to do those same essential things; but it is a still different, and a much less satisfying, thing for a person with broader horizons to be expected to spend her life doing nonessential things for her family. The name of the job is the same, but the job itself has changed from carrying water to making lemonade.

Closely related to the nature of the mother's job is the fact of public schooling. There was a day when a large part of raising children was teaching them the things they needed to know. Besides the basics of reading and writing, parents had to teach their girls to be home-makers and their boys to do something by which they could earn a living. None of this education in the home is essential any longer. Schools teach most of the basics and the practical knowledge that isn't gained at school can be gotten from library books. Education in the family is now limited to moral and religious education, and, while those are extremely important, teaching them is not a full-time job.

The rise of technology and the factory system has gradually removed from the home, and therefore from women, any important function except child care. The frontier mother had the entire brewing, food preparation, education, weaving, textile- and garment-making industries under her control. She ran, in effect, a small business with all the responsibilities and decision-making that go into such a project. She was a housewife but she was *not* a dependent. From that busy and responsible life women have been moved to one which confines them to the company of only small children many hours a day and to repetitive tasks.

In summary, family life today is not what it was even fifty years ago. Because of the immense changes in our society, the roles of family members are quite different from what they once were. Women are not doing what women did a hundred years ago, children are not being raised as they used to be, fathers are not playing the same part in their children's lives that fathers once did. We must face those facts of contemporary life and be willing to make the necessary adjustments.

Christians should be sure that the changes they make in family life are toward the building up of the family unit, toward increasing the family's ability to achieve its goals of growth and emotional support for each member. Ironically, the feminists, who care so little about the future of the family, are demanding some changes that would build up the family, changes that Christians should be wholeheartedly supporting: that the burden of child care be shared by others than the mother (as it always was until very recently); and that fathers should play a much larger and more active role in the raising of the children.

3. The Use of Women's Talents

Of all the goals of women's liberation, the one most important to feminists is precisely the one Christians should be most eager to accept, the desire to let each woman decide what she will do with her life, what her talents are, where her unique services will be in this world, without pressuring her into accepting the role of wife and mother as definitive of her future.

For too long girls have been encouraged to believe that once they marry, they need no longer worry about how to spend their time or what to do with their lives. The fallacy that keeping a husband happy is sufficient contribution to the world, regardless of how talented the woman may be, has been too long accepted.

One need not believe that every housewife has the ability to be a brain surgeon or an astrophysicist to see that the abilities girls demonstrate in college seem to disappear when they have been housewives for a few years. The writers stop writing, the communications majors stop running radio programs, the drama majors give up acting or set design or production, the artists stop producing, the scientists leave their laboratories, the teachers their classrooms, the philosophers their books. Very few women who are wives and mothers are also seriously committed to goals of another kind.

The female with musical ability will give a few piano lessons, perhaps, and sing in the church choir, perhaps even direct it, but she will be unusual if she considers music a career equal in importance to that of motherhood. The woman with interest in theology may continue to do some reading, and may lead women's groups in Bible study, but she will never consider herself a theologian, or take seriously the possibility that she may have a contribution to make to the theology of her church.

The talents of such women are being wasted. If Christians take seriously Matthew 25, they know that it is an act of disobedience to God to allow one's talents to be wasted or hidden. Yet very few individual Christians and even fewer churches recognize that the demand to grow and develop and use one's gifts applies as much to women as to men.

In allowing such abilities to go unused, the church is depriving itself of a source of leadership and growth, a deprivation that it cannot afford. When church leadership is left entirely to men, the church often suffers from the lack of time those men have to devote to its cause. If the men do take adequate time for church work, their families often suffer neglect. Some wives, on the other hand, have more time than their husbands for outside-the-home activities and could therefore do better than the men some of the jobs in the church. Instead, these capable people, because they are women, are confined to menial tasks, many of which are unnecessary to the church's function.

Feminists protest the failure of women to develop their abilities and to take seriously their own identities, because they think such women are not living fully, are not becoming fully human, or are not getting as much out of life as they ought. Christians should equally protest, partly because this situation wastes human talent, but even more because such women are not giving all that they could to the development of God's kingdom.

Even if one believes that a mother must spend ten hours a day at home when her children are small, homemaking still is not the lifetime career it once was. With small families women may have full-time work for ten years, with large families, even twenty. That still leaves many years in which a woman could do the essentials of housekeeping in a few hours a week. If her husband were to share that work, she could do it in even less. Those twenty to twenty-five years that are left to women after their children no longer need them now are often wasted. Some women go back to work, but it is frequently menial work incommensurate with their training and ability. Some women even go back to serious, highly skilled careers, but always with the lurking feeling that this is secondary to their more important role of wife and mother.

Christians must take seriously Paul's vision of the church as one body in which each member has a part to play. Nothing in that vision suggests that women must be all hands or hearts. Women can be feet and lungs and brains and muscles in the church just as surely as men can.

Concretely, Christians must start immediately to help young women see that they need to plan their lives beyond their wedding day. They must be told that their responsibilities to the church are not met by their husbands. Neither are their responsibilities limited to teaching the small children in Sunday school. Women must be helped to plan for a future beyond the children, to use those years when motherhood is not a full-time job.

Young women should be encouraged to think of their careers as a part of their future equal in importance with marriage and motherhood. Those whose careers demand long training or who could not easily break off their careers for some years to raise children should be encouraged to think about possibilities of half-time employment for husband and wife or about what kind of mother substitute would be adequate and available. Those whose careers are such that interruptions of a few years would not be serious may think in terms of taking some years off to be at home with small children. At least one young couple I know is thinking in terms of the husband's taking off for a few years since he is less satisfied with his job than is the wife. Some fortunate women may find that their careers allow part-time work during the young-mother years. Once it has been established that women should think of themselves as having serious work besides motherhood, the means of implementing that commitment are many and can be varied to meet the needs of different jobs, different-size families, and different women.

Just as serious as the waste of talent that occurs among women is the demeaning attitude toward themselves that is fostered by their failure to keep growing. Especially, it seems to me, some Christian women have a very low opinion of themselves. Many of them, on reading this material, will feel that talk of talents being hidden or the kingdom being deprived of their work is grandiose, that they have no talents or gifts sufficient to be concerned about. That is not true, of course. From one perspective, it is even an insult to God, for He has created each of us, has given each of us talents, and has said that every member of the church is of value to it, that each has a job to perform.

It is difficult to document the lack of self-esteem among women, but many, many observers have seen it. Women consistently feel that their work, whatever it is, is less important than their husband's. They feel they are being selfish if they insist on doing their own work while their husbands babysit. They think a husband's time is more valuable than their own and that therefore husbands ought not be bothered with mundane tasks like washing dishes. They think, in spite of all the talk about the importance and difficulty of motherhood, that husbands work harder than wives. In individual cases any one or all of the above beliefs may be accurate, of course. It may be true in some cases that the husband's work is genuinely more important than the wife's or that he works harder than she. But it is not *always* true. And it is *never* true that his work or his time or his convenience is more important than the continuing growth and development of the wife. Christians should understand that *each* person — male or female — is equally valuable and equally entitled to growth and to satisfying work.

Feminists push careers, which they define as paid work in the economy, for women. Christians should push careers for women, too, but Christians should be aware of the many possibilities that

84

exist for unpaid careers. If a Christian woman can be of service to her God and her fellow humans in a job that her society will not pay for, that career is not of less value than a paid one.

Women should be encouraged to think of their work as a serious commitment to some goal. Their volunteer efforts should not be limited to scattered bits and pieces of help to others, none of which have any real goal or future. Women should be encouraged to take on jobs, whether paid or not, that offer the possibilities for growth, for learning, for developing themselves. They should spend their child-raising years preparing for future responsibilities and leadership opportunities. Christians should never fall victim to the belief that only paid work is worth doing. Neither should they believe that dozens of minor and scattered volunteer efforts will give the satisfaction and growth that a sustained, purposeful effort toward some goal will give. The first chapters of Genesis make very clear that God intended humans to work, not just at easy, quickly accomplished tasks, however necessary, but at difficult, sustained jobs that demand all of one's resources and energy. That kind of work is too seldom asked of women.

In encouraging women to seek careers outside the home, feminists are chiefly interested in removing from women their status as dependents. Both legally and psychologically, married women are treated in our society not as equal workers with their husbands but as dependents whom the man must support. Thus the hard-working young mother is told that she owes certain things to her husband because he is "earning" the money, as if her work was not equally a way of "earning" certain rewards.

Christians should have a better realization than non-Christians that dependence is not a state to be shunned, that in fact it is the state of all human creatures before God and other people. We are all dependents—on God for sure and on our society as well. But Christians cannot work that argument both ways. Either being a dependent is shameful or it is not shameful. The sex of the dependent and the provider are immaterial.

Christians also should not try to work the money argument from both ends. Young women who wish to work are told that Christians should not feel that earning money is the only criterion for success in the world. But the man who puts his job before his family because he wants to earn more money, or the man who wants certain privileges granted him because he "brings home the bacon," is belying that statement. For men, we believe that earning money gives them certain rights, for women, earning money must never be considered important.

The wife who says "I wish I had my own money to spend" is revealing a perfectly normal desire for independence and the freedom to make her own decisions. Such desires are a part of being an adult; no grown person likes to feel that every decision he makes is subject to review by a higher human authority. We recognize this principle with children by giving them more and more decision-making authority over their own lives as they grow older. We recognize it for women until they marry; then suddenly every expenditure, every decision about using her time must be submitted to her husband. It is no wonder if she grows restive under this kind of dependence, a kind that even adolescents, for the most part, are free of.

The double standard toward the earning of money appears most often when there is conflict in the marriage over how to spend money. If the wife wants new furniture and the husband wants a new car, the husband is all too likely to take the position that because he earns the money, he is entitled to decide how to spend it. Such an argument belies the statements made in other contexts that the wife's work is just as important as the husband's, that her role happens to be at home and his out in the world but both have equal right to the results of their mutual labors. If we want to reinforce that belief, we might insist that checks earned by men who have wives engaged in mothering be made out to both husband and wife, as are the income tax refunds from joint returns.

Such a minor change in our legal practices would help to remind us that the work wives do at home really is the other half of the work their husbands do elsewhere.

4. Marriage

The possibility of a woman's making a serious commitment to work outside the home, whether that work is paid or unpaid, brings up the entire problem of the marriage relationship. One reason wives are so reluctant to take on responsible work outside the home is that such work may necessitate the husband taking on certain chores that he resents. He might have to cook dinner, or babysit, or spend an evening alone more often than he likes. Many a husband has come to think of his wife as a kind of personal valet, a person whose *job* it is to be helpful and available whenever she is wanted. I submit that such a view of marriage is not Christian.

Dorothy Sayers once wrote (*Gaudy Night*) that most men consider themselves to be their wives' jobs, but that a few rare ones see themselves not as jobs but as fellow creatures. Christian men should not see themselves as jobs, as masters to be waited on, as lords to be served, as beings who are to be "taken care of" by their wives, but as members of a partnership in which each partner is called to serve God with the help of the other. Christian marriage is not man serving God and woman serving man, but man serving God and woman serving God, each helping the other. The members of this partnership bring each other their concerns, their worries, their failures, their successes, their sense of inadequacy, their needs, and by sharing them, relieve the burdens and increase the joys. Such a view of marriage would not prevent women from making commitments to tasks outside the home, would not make looking after husbands such a time- and energy-consuming chore that serious work outside was impossible.

A problem that many foresee in a family where husband and wife both have career interests is that of whose career takes precedence. When the husband gets a job offer in a distant city and the wife's job in this city is satisfying to her, or vice versa, what happens? This is a real problem for couples who have such equal careers, and the more the goals of women's liberation are met, the more widespread the problem will be. It is not insurmountable, however, and attacking the problem with Christian principles should make it easier to solve.

In the first place, Christians should be able to turn down promotions and positions offering more prestige with less of a pang than their non-Christian colleagues. Christians do not always in fact feel this way, but they should, for Christians should understand better than other people that success in life is not dependent upon how much money one makes or how prestigious one's position is. Furthermore, Christians understand that one can be of service in any position, and the degree of one's service to fellow humans is the real criterion of successful life.

Even with such principles firmly in mind, however, difficulties will arise. One partner in the marriage may be offered a position that offers greater opportunity for service, or greater development of his talents. Somebody is going to have to give up something. For Christian marriage partners who are genuinely concerned about their mates, the decision should not be an impossible one. Ideally, the conflict should result from each one's wanting to do what is best for the other, but I do not suppose it will work out that way in reality. The point, however, is that when Christians realize that careers are not the most important thing in life to either partner, and also realize that each partner has equal right to development and opportunity, that should make the decision easier than it would be if both people had their own career success as the chief goal in life.

Accepting the goals of feminism as one's own goals will demand a radical shift in one's view of the marriage relationship. Traditionally Christians have seen the wife's job as being chiefly to keep her husband happy. Christians have conceived of her service as being to her *husband*, and through him to God. But if a woman's talents are of such a nature that she chooses service outside the home, her relationship to her husband will change. Her chief goal in life will no longer be to keep him happy; it will be to do her work well. That does not mean she may neglect him, of course, any more than his work allows him to neglect her. But it will demand a reshaping of expectations.

The typical vision of marriage is of a couple with one job—his career. The husband works directly on that, the wife indirectly, by keeping him happy (and sometimes by entertaining, acting as secretary, whatever). Feminists have a different vision. They see a marriage as made up of two people each of whom has a job in the world. She does her job, he does his, and each returns to the marriage relationship for support and sustenance. Sometimes the woman's job (or one hopes in the future, the man's) may be the raising of the children and the keeping of the house, but even in that case, her job ought not be to act as an adjunct to her husband, but to raise the children. Hence, when her children no longer need her, she can find another job. Feminists tend to see this model of marriage as the only acceptable one.

Christians may want to disagree. They may feel that the old pattern, where the woman's job was to help in her husband's job, is still a good one. But Christians cannot, I think, any longer insist that that pattern is the only one possible in a Christian marriage. Given the size of our families and homes, and the organization in our society for supplying food and educating children, it is quite possible for Christians to have a marriage in which two people each have a job in the world, sharing equally the responsibilities for the support of the family, the care of the home, and the raising of the children.

There was a day when raising children and keeping house was such a huge task that somebody in each family had to devote full time to it. There was a day when the wife could be an equal partner in the family job—farming and family-owned businesses, for example. There are still a few jobs that permit such partnerships —young couples who work together on the mission field, for example, or who together set up and run a business. But for most people the day of equal partnerships between husband and wife is past. When the children no longer need their mother, she is without a job—except that very part-time one of keeping house. Christians should consider, I think, whether it is really Christian stewardship to suggest that such women spend the rest of their lives tending their husbands. Christians should insist that such women should have some work—paid or unpaid, done at home or at an office, full- or part-time—that stimulates them, uses their talents, contributes to the kingdom, and keeps them growing.

Christian women have always been reluctant to make demands, partly because the whole teaching of Christianity, especially for women, is that quiet service is proper. If one must do positive damage to others in order to win his own rights, Christians should certainly prefer to sacrifice their own rights. However, meeting the goals of the women's movement need not do any permanent or severe damage to men or to the family. It may inconvenience some men; it may cause a somewhat painful readjustment of expectations between men and women; it may even cause temporary hostility between formerly peaceful marriage partners. But none of those things need be the cause of permanent damage, and most of them can, if approached with Christian love and with a firm grasp of Christian principles, become the means for building marriages and families that are closer to Christian ideals.

5. Sexual Attitudes

American sexual attitudes toward women are best represented by two national images: Miss America and the *Playboy* bunny. Miss America is beautiful and charming in a superficial way. She has some talent, but she is not an expert in her field. By the admission of the pageant's sponsors, she is judged two-thirds on looks (bathing suit and evening gown competition), and one-third on talent. In reality, of course, even the talent of a Beethoven could never compensate for such minor visual flaws as a crooked leg or a somewhat overlarge nose. In short, looks are necessary; talent is only desirable. Miss America has perfect measurements, speaks sweetly and unaggressively, and has no abrasive views on anything. *Playboy* bunnies are simply the same girls gone promiscuous. They, too, must first of all be visually perfect and must not hold abrasive views (though they are sometimes allowed to express liberal establishment views in a quiet way). In short, Americans want above all that their women be good-looking.

And Christians are almost as guilty of this as any other Americans. They admire Miss America, even bring her to speak to young people's groups if she happens to be a Christian. They do not protest the pageant in spite of its gross use of young women to sell products and make money for the pageant's sponsors. They do not protest the parading of women's bodies in public, as if women were so many cattle or slaves up for inspection. They do, of course, protest the *Playboy* image because that image is too sexual. But about the emphasis on looks, the neglect of anything that reveals intellect or humanness or serious commitment to something, they are no more concerned than anyone else.

Sadly enough, it has been feminists, not Christians, who have protested this view of womanhood in our society. Christians have seldom been bothered by the blatant use of sex appeal to sell products, except when the sex was too explicit. They have been unconcerned about the extreme emphasis on looks and youth that our society imposes on women. They have even, to some extent, accepted it for themselves, being almost as unable as their non-Christian counterparts to appreciate a good, unselfish, able woman who is homely and middle-aged. Among Christians, as among non-Christians, women spend immense time and money on their appearance—their hair, their clothes, their cosmetics, their perfumes. Although the standard for good looks among Christian women is somewhat more modest and restrained than elsewhere in our society, the emphasis is the same: women must look good.

That women should be neat and clean and modestly dressed (as should men) is not at issue here. The point is the tremendous concern with looks, a concern that ought to be of less importance to Christians than to other people because Christians believe that internal qualities are of more importance than external appearance.

In other ways, too, Christians have absorbed the sexual mores of their society instead of the values Christianity teaches. The most blatant example of this is the failure on the part of the church, and often on the part of Christian parents, to teach their sons their responsibility to the girls they date. Girls are taught early to resist aggressive males, to protect their virginity, to make sure they are married before they give themselves to a man. And boys are allowed to believe that such aggressive demands on girls are legitimate, that it is her, not his, business to protect her virginity. Young men will be called to account for sexual immorality only if the girl becomes pregnant. If they manage to avoid that error their sexual exploits will be considered the "sowing of wild oats."

Girls are taught an equally damaging view of sex when they are encouraged to treat their bodies as something they trade away to a man in return for the security of marriage or, sometimes, in return for his affection and attention before marriage. "If you loved me, you'd let me," he says, and she, anxious to keep him, finally accepts his reasoning and gives in. Then, of course, she feels he "owes" her marriage. Young people seem now to be talking more openly about their sexual feelings, but their relationships are no more honest, it seems to me, than they were before. Girls are still being victimized by boys who will make no commitments to them, and the girls are still victimizing boys by trapping them into marriage through sexual means. This mutual exploitation view of sexual relationships must be replaced by one which encourages each party to see the other as a person, a creature to whom responsibilities are owed and whose welfare is important.

Although they have seen the exploitative nature of many contemporary sexual attitudes, feminists have not realized that *whenever* the sexual act is separated from commitment to another person, that act will be exploitative most of the time. When a person is unwilling to commit himself to another person—unwilling to care for that person, watch out for his welfare, make that person's life good to whatever extent he can — then he will almost certainly see the relationship largely, or entirely, as one from which he is getting something. When he stops getting whatever satisfaction the relationship provides, he will end the relationship, regardless of what such action may do to the partner. Without the promise of accepting someone for better or for worse, the relationship will be based on "getting something," rather than on "giving something."

Furthermore, any relationship that has no promise of permanency in it can never be an open one. Open relationships are difficult to achieve anyhow, but one cannot even begin if he knows that at any moment the partner may end the relationship. How can one reveal weakness or ask for help when one can't be sure of the reception? Without commitment from his partner, a person's moves toward genuine intimacy and sharing must necessarily be tentative, quickly withdrawn if it appears that they are irritating or threatening the partner.

Most feminists, then, have accepted the pleasure principle of sex—that the only thing sex offers is enjoyment—that pervades our society. Christians must resist that view of sexual relationships, and insist that the sex act is intimately bound up with the decision of two people to commit themselves to each other, to share each other's burdens, to love (not in the romantic, but in the Biblical *agape* sense) each other until death.

Feminists, Germaine Greer (*The Female Eunuch*) in particular, have further declared that our society insists on desexing women. Christians should consider whether they have, in the past at least, denied the sexual nature of women, whether they have presented the idea that nice, Christian girls have no sexual desires or needs, that they don't really care about sex at all. If Christians have taught this view, or are still teaching it, they must realize that such a view is false, and probably contributes to frigidity and guilt feelings in Christian women.

An attitude that many Christian young men suffer from may also be partially the fault of the church. Many Christian men find it difficult to combine the ideal of wife and mother and the image of a sexual partner. Such young men tend to see young women as either bed partners or candidates for marriage, not as both. The Roman Catholic Church has been charged with perpetrating this division by its emphasis on the virgin mother, thereby increasing the contrast between the mother image and the sexual partner image. Wherever the blame for this attitude lies, Christians should be working to overcome it and to teach the Biblical view of sexual relationships and the sexuality of women.

Both the denial of women's sexuality and the separation of motherhood from sex are partially traceable, I think, to the attitude among some Christians that sex is dirty or indecent. Christians should be able to face the sexual nature of men and women without having to act as if men are brutes and women are victims. The suggestion sometimes made in Christian circles that the sex act was not instituted until after the fall is a symptom of this unfortunate view. The response of Adam to the arrival of Eve in his life (as translated in the New English Bible) seems to me to be one of the great love poems of all time: "Now this, at last—bone from my bones, flesh from my flesh!—this shall be called woman." Freely translated, Adam is saying, "Here at last is a creature with whom I can be physically one—how glorious!"

The other side of the Miss America coin in our society is the image of the real man as virile, active, strong, muscled, athletic, aggressive, and totally independent. Christians must agree with the feminists that this is not a healthy image for men to have of themselves nor for women to have of men. It is unhealthy because it emphasizes qualities that are ill suited to producing Christian virtues and because it denies the variety of men's abilities and needs. The Christian emphasis on humility, service, gentleness, love, concern for others is directly contrary to what Americans think a man should be. Men have, as a result, a conflict in knowing what goals to seek for themselves, and unfortunately they far too often choose the American rather than the Christian goals. Women, too, often prefer "masculine" men to Christian men.

Sexual prowess is the defining feature of masculinity in our society. The most damaging thing an American man can admit to is sexual impotence or disinterest. So closely have masculinity and sexual power become identified in our society that many men see any challenge from a woman—any threat to their ability, their authority, their prestige—as a sexual threat. Even our street language reflects that attitude. Yet such a belief that a man must be sexually aggressive in order to be "masculine" is thoroughly un-Christian.

Furthermore, masculinity is equated with aggressiveness and force of personality in a way that is un-Christian. How many Christians would really admire Jesus if He were to appear among us washing feet and meekly submitting to the authorities? We much prefer Peter with his aggressive demands and his urge to have his own way.

I do not mean to make Jesus the quiet, meek figure He appears in far too many Sunday school illustrations. He must have been a person with great charm, great charisma, great ability to attract people. But I'm afraid our recent moves to "masculinize" Him have little to do with a desire to see Him as He was, and are more an attempt to make Him conform to our image of what a man should be. Had Jesus appeared in the twentieth century, I cannot believe He would have been a professional football player or an aggressive businessman. He was far more concerned with serving than with His own prestige; He was more worried about the needs of His people than about His own position; He did not equate masculinity with muscles, authoritarian rule, sexual prowess, or strength. He wept publicly; He took time for women and children; He spoke gently, though firmly, to His betrayer; He refused to use force or violence.

The American image of the male denies, furthermore, the variety among men, just as the image of the female denies the variety among women. Many men are not aggressive by nature, they are not insistent, demanding, or domineering. Many men have no great desire to make a name for themselves, or to "succeed." Many have no interest in the "masculine" pursuits of athletics, hunting, mechanics. They like music, perhaps, or poetry. They may be gentle, mild people, who prefer following to leading and listening to talking.

Just as many women are stunted by their society's refusal to let them grow in their natural abilities, many men are forced to assume attitudes and roles that are uncomfortable for them. They are being forced to pretend that they are something they are not.

Christians should rid themselves of these American stereotypes; they should hold the view of individuals that Scripture teaches: that male and female are both part of God's image, that each of us reflects God no matter how "feminine" or "masculine" each is, that each person has a unique work to do in the kingdom and the ability to do it.

In many important matters involving sex, Christians cannot accept the beliefs of most feminists (nor of most of American society); Christians cannot see sexual intercourse as *only* a pleasurable experience, nor can they deny the need for permanency in sexual relationships. But in the matter of destroying sexual stereotypes Christians ought to be in the front ranks of the battle, for the current images of what is "feminine" or "masculine" stunt the growth of women and make the practice of Christian virtues more difficult for men.

Conclusion

Non-Christian feminists and Christians must part ways on certain basic issues, the most basic of which is their different beliefs about the purpose of human life. Most feminists believe that a person's ultimate goal should be to find self-fulfillment, identity, or personal satisfaction, whatever phrase one wants to use. Christians, on the other hand, believe that the goal of life is service to God and other people. That difference in their ultimate commitment explains most of the differences between them: their differences about the nature of sexual relationships, for example, and the more serious commitment to marriage that Christians ought to have.

But the concept of service for a Christian woman has been too long used to keep many Christian women from the kind of service for which they are best suited. The fact that one *can* surely serve God in the role of housewife and mother does not imply that every married woman must do so. Furthermore, the concept of service to other people has been too restricted for Christian women. Women have been thought to have very few or very minor obligations to anyone outside the family, while men have been assumed to have very important obligations in the church, in the community, in the world. But according to Genesis 1, man and woman were both given the command to "fill the earth, subdue, rule over every living thing." The command was not that man should rule and woman stand quietly in the background to support him when necessary. They were both to rule.

Many Christians hold another belief that sets them seriously apart from the feminists: the conviction that women are basically different from men in ways that unfit them for the kind of work men do. I have tried to show throughout this book that there is not enough evidence, either Scriptural or scientific, for believing that women and men are inherently different. Furthermore, even if they were different, none of the traditional beliefs about their roles follow from the premise of their differences. Whatever the differences may be; they do not unfit women for playing the same roles as men in contemporary society.

Some Christians argue that Scripture shows women are intended to be mates, mothers, and homemakers, period. I have tried to show that the Scriptural evidence is, at best, ambiguous on this point, and that the past functions of women were, in fact, quite unlike the functions they are asked to perform today.

I believe that one of the meanings of Genesis 1-3 is that the fall into sin seriously distorted the relationships between men and women. And the most serious distortion was reflected in the curse on woman: "Your desire shall be to your husband and he shall reign over you."

The worst elements in that reign have been eliminated in the Western world. Men are no longer allowed to sell their wives, as they once were; women are no longer the property of their husbands; they no longer disappear legally when they marry; they no longer are refused the means of self-support; they no longer are denied education; they no longer are refused full citizenship in their nation. But some elements of that misused authority are still with us. The effects are seen in the distortion of sexual relationships into a mutually exploitative arrangement, and in the denial to women of the freedom to develop freely and fully their natural abilities. Men, too, have suffered from the insistence on the "differences" between men and women, from the sexual exploitation, and, perhaps above all in American society, from the financial exploitation that lays on them the whole burden of support for a family. Perhaps most serious of all, the family is breaking down under the pressure of applying old role definitions to new conditions.

To the feminist insistence on freedom of choice for each individual, Christians must add the need for responsible choice, and the insistence that such choices be made in accord with God's will. Much of my argument in this book, especially in the second chapter, has been aimed at showing that some of the choices advocated by the feminists are not contrary to God's will.

Christians must part company with the mainstream of feminism on certain basic goals, but on some things they can agree. All talents given by God should be developed and used, all lives should be meaningful, all people should have satisfying and worthwhile work, work commensurate with their abilities. Greater freedom from sexual stereotypes, greater freedom in choosing roles, will not gain these things for all members of our society, but it will help to gain them for a significant portion of our population—all those men and women who do not fit, or fit only with discomfort, into the molds prescribed for them by our sexual prejudices.